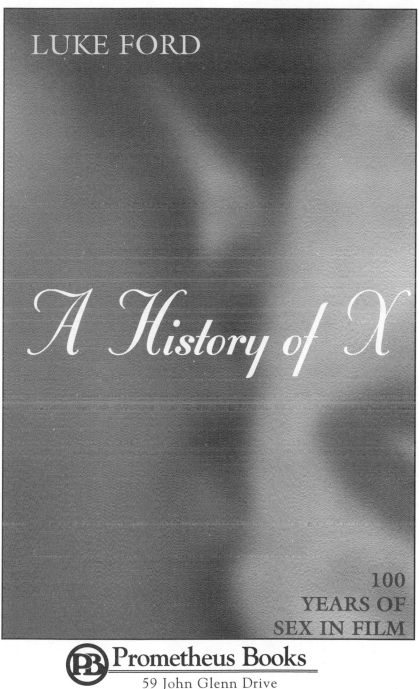

LUKE FORD

A History of X

100
YEARS OF
SEX IN FILM

Prometheus Books
59 John Glenn Drive
Amherst, New York 14228-2197

Published 1999 by Prometheus Books

Inquiries should be addressed to
Prometheus Books, 59 John Glenn Drive, Amherst, New York 14228–2197.
VOICE: 716–691–0133, ext. 207. FAX: 716–564–2711.
WWW.PROMETHEUSBOOKS.COM

03 02 01 00 99   5 4 3 2 1

Library of Congress Cataloging-in-Publication Data

Ford, Luke.
    A history of X : 100 years of sex in film / by Luke Ford.
        p.   cm.
    Includes bibliographical references.
    ISBN 1–57392–678–7 (cl. : alk. paper)
    1. Erotic films—History and criticism. I. Title.
PN1995.9.S45F67   1999
791.43'6538—dc21   99–12084
                                                                CIP

Printed in the United States of America on acid-free paper

Contents

Preface

Though Americans spend billions of dollars on pornography, most of us know little about the industry that strokes our deepest fantasies. "Some day there will be big fat books," predicted porn director William Rotsler in 1973, "with titles like *Early Porno, The Love Directors, Stars of the Golden Age of Pornopix, The Films of Marilyn Chambers, How Deep Throat Was Made. . . .*" He couldn't have been more wrong. Despite porn's proliferation, nobody wrote anything close to what Rotsler prophesied.

For the past two years, I've ventured into virgin territory to write the first comprehensive history of porn. My book fleshes out the one hundred years of explicit sex in movies, concentrating on the quarter century since *Deep Throat* when porn joined popular culture.

Why read about porn? To learn about yourself and the world. The industry provides a superb testing ground for finding out what men want. (Female demand for porn expressed in dollars spent is insignificant.) Unless pornographers satisfy the needs of millions, they go bankrupt. While Ph.D.s theorize about sexuality, pornographers deal with its reality. By studying porn, therefore, we are more likely to study something substantial than if we undertook graduate work in sociology. The sex industry grosses billions of dollars each year by appealing to the male daydream, to what motivates many of us to get out of bed in the morning and go to work. Revolving around lust and money, porn springs from the most primal desires.

Pornographers, to varying degrees, live out the fantasies that haunt millions. By delving deep inside the lives porn stars, one can discover the results of getting what you want. Does fame, fortune, and fucking lead to happiness? The lives of such "actresses" as Marilyn Chambers, Ginger Lynn, and Savannah provide differing answers.

That you picked up this book and read thus far indicates you probably agree that to ignore porn is to ignore life, to avoid facing dreams made flesh. These dreams are not pretty. Males learn quickly that few females and the religious will explore pornographic visions. A lad who wants to win friends and influence people does not discuss his fantasies in mixed company. While women complain that men refuse to open up, men know that to voice what they truly think about invites shock, derision, and anger.

Women who seek to understand men should rent a few X-rated videos—say, *Anal Analysis*. That's what your loving father, husband, brother, and friend ponder: *Anal Analysis. Women Who Suck Cock and Eat Cum. Black Fuckers.*

I'm sorry I had to be the one to give the bad news.

Porn acts out our dirty desires. It does the things we can't do, such as screw the neighbor's wife. Videos like *Anal Destroyer* do not create man in their image as much as men create *Anal Destroyer*. Eliminating sex for entertainment, however beneficial, will not destroy the penis—the ultimate source of the "porno plague." That virtually all men in all cultures in all of history desired infinite variety of sex partners and raped en masse when they could get away with it debunks the notion that Hugh Hefner created promiscuity.

Most of my friends and the religious community passionately oppose my decision to research porn. At best, they think it odd; at worst, evil. So why did I do it? To stroke my two greatest interests—myself and the world. By exploring porn I explore myself. I explore the fantasies I rarely utter. And by understanding those fantasies, I feel more at peace.

Through understanding the sex industry I better understand humanity. It's wonderful to desire a better world, but first you must face reality. If you don't get your premises right, your crusade may do more harm than good. Understanding that porn springs from male desire more than male desire springs from porn would save thousands of activists from wasting their time. Their focus is wrong. To modify a quote from Shakespeare, our problems are not in our stars, or in our porn, but in ourselves. Inanimate objects like videos or guns or nuclear weapons do not cause evil, Jewish theologian and KABC talk show host Dennis Prager notes repeatedly. People do. If a man remains single all his life because he will only settle down with a *Playboy* Playmate, that is his fault, not porn's.

Two men have greatly shaped my opinion of porn: Dennis Prager and late UCLA psychiatrist Dr. Robert Stoller.

I thank *Adult Video News* and Knight Publishing for allowing me to quote from their copyrighted magazines. Out of the hundreds of persons I talked to in the course of researching this book, the following were particularly helpful: critics Roger T. Pipe, Sheldon Ranz, and Pat Riley; journalists Michael Louis Albo, Jared Rutter, Paul Fishbein, Wally Wharton, and Hart Williams; members of the rec.arts. movies.erotica (RAME) newsgroup Craig Anthony, the Director, Imperator, and Brad Williams; and pornographers Jim Holliday, Bill Margold, Cash Markman, and Ron Vogel.

I dedicate this book to my buddies Rob, Joe, and Barbara Spallone.

1.

Naked Came the Stranger

"Pornography" denotes writings and pictures intended to stimulate lust through the explicit portrayal of sex. Discussions of sex in academic works, for example, may be explicit, but are not pornographic because they do not seek to arouse. And while a TV program may be arousing, it is not pornographic if it is not explicit. A subcategory of pornography, "porn" refers to the commercial product of the X-rated industry: photos and movies of adults performing sexual intercourse.

In the popular mind, "pornography" connotes explicit images that exploit women while "erotica" refers to nonexploitive, less explicit images. For example, *Hustler*'s Larry Flynt produces pornography while novelist Janet Daily produces erotica. The moral-legal term "obscenity" reinforces the designation "pornography."

The English word "pornography" is a combination of two Greek words: *porne*, meaning "harlot," and *grapheim*, meaning "to write." First listed in the *Oxford English Dictionary* in 1857, "pornography" literally means "writing about whores."

For as long as humans have been able to draw or write, they've crafted pornography. Danish sociologist Berl Kutchinsky traces the beginnings of modern porn to the publication of three books anonymously authored in the 1650s: *The Wayward Prostitute, Girls School,* and *Satya.* Translated into the major languages, they became the models for later pornographic books and movies. An examination of the three classics shows that little has changed in porn over the past 350 years. Themes of lesbianism, sodomy, seduction, multiple copulation, flagellation, and sadism dominate, writes Kutchinsky, "as well as total amorality, a disregard for artistic merit, an absence of affection or other emotions, flimsy plots, stereotyped characterizations, monotonous repetitiousness, and a constant exaggeration of sexual interest, energy and potency."[1]

By the Victorian era, sexually explicit fiction had developed into a mature literary genre increasingly defined by its illegality. When Sir Charles Sedley in 1663 got drunk in a public tavern, climbed upstairs, took off all his clothes, and urinated onto the crowded street below, he provoked the first recorded occasion in Anglo-Saxon jurisprudence that the state punished an affront to public decency. Until this time, most Western societies worried more about blasphemy than obscenity. After the seventeenth century and the Enlightenment, however, porn and censorship grew hand-in-hand. Common law, as opposed to ecclesiastical, began to apply to obscene libel in England.

"Pornography heralds the increasing hostility of the artist toward society," write Al Di Lauro and Gerald Rabkin in their 1976 book, *Dirty Movies.*[2] Sexual license in literature, for instance, led to explicit attacks on religion. By the eighteenth century, porn depicted sexual orgies in religious orders. This rebellious attitude reached its apogee in the Marquis de Sade, who fleshed out what lies behind porn's obsessional detail: "the superiority of the senses to established moral codes." Di Lauro and Rabkin go on to describe de Sade as "the clearest, most powerful example of the pornographer as transgressor."[3]

Still photography was invented in 1827 and motion pictures in 1894. Five minutes after each invention, quips producer David Friedman, a woman posed naked before the latest male toy. Actress Louise Willy disrobes in the 1896 French film *Le Bain*, the earliest known sex film. Other French flicks before the turn of the century offered similar fare while in Germany, producer Oskar Messter revealed women taking off their clothes while exercising, dancing, or bathing.

As with the development of other forms of communication, such as writing, drawing, painting, and printing, pornographers led the way in the popular application of moving pictures. They made sex films known as "stags." As an adjective, "stag" means "for men only." Thus a stag film is a film for men only—a film depicting graphic sex. Stag films frequently appeared at stag parties—parties for men only.

America probably made the most stag films, followed by France, where the genre originated and flourished until Gaullist repression in the 1950s. Becoming so adept at making stags that the term "French film" became synonymous with porn, French pornographers developed many of the genre's basic plots, which William Rotsler listed as the following:

1. A woman alone becomes aroused after handling a phallic-shaped object. Masturbation follows. A man arrives, is invited inside, sexual play begins.

2. A farm girl gets excited watching animals copulate. She runs into a farmhand, or a traveling salesman, and sexual play begins.
3. A doctor begins examining a woman and sexual play begins.
4. A burglar finds a girl in bed or rapes her or vice versa.
5. A sunbather or skinny dipper gets caught and seduced.[4]

Latin American stags came largely from the brothels of Tijuana and Havana and bestiality appears in some, such as *Rin Tin Tin Mexicano*, *A Hunter and His Dog*, *Rascal Rex*, and *Mexican Dog*. Technically abysmal, these humiliating productions focus their hatred on women and the Catholic Church. Films such as *Mexican Honeymoon* show priests exploiting their parishioners. Anti-Catholic porn flourished in countries where the Church dominated. By contrast, American stags skirted religion. "I would rather my kid saw a stag film than *The Ten Commandments*," said comic Lenny Bruce, "because I don't want my kid to kill Christ when he comes back. Pleasure is a dirty word in Christian culture. Pleasure is Satan's word."[5]

Satanic pleasure fills the classic 1907 stag from Argentina, *El Sartorio*, which begins with three women playing in a river. A man dressed as a devil with a tail, horns, and false whiskers emerges out of the foliage and captures one woman. She sucks him off, engages in a 69, and finally screws him. Close-up shots of his penis pushing inside her appear every few seconds.

Stag films specialized in such "meat shots," close-ups of penetration, rather than "money (cum) shots," men ejaculating on, rather than within, women. By the early 1970s, however, cum shots became so essential to porn that it seemed flicks without them weren't pornographic.

American fare, such as 1915's *A Free Ride*, emphasized sex over story. Shot outside using many camera angles and titles, *Ride* (the first known American stag) flows from the open films of the first decade of the century. The story is simple. A man picks up two girls and takes them for a drive in the country. He stops the car in a wooded area, gets out, and walks behind a bush to urinate. The girls spy on him, become aroused, and sex ensues. Unconsciously, *A Free Ride* reveals a classic male-female parallel: What urination is to women, the release of a biological need, sex is to men. For most of us males, most of the time, orgasm most resembles a strong piss down the toilet.

America's thriving underground stag film industry came under attack in the 1920s from law enforcement and U.S. Post Office agents. Porn commentators, good liberals all, blame socioeconomic structures for freezing the form of the stag film at the point achieved in its infancy in *A Free Ride*. But almost a century later, in the era of greatest freedom humanity has ever known, porn remains a limited genre. Just as adult films began with arty movies like *The Devil in Miss Jones* and *The Opening of Misty Beethoven* before dropping such pretensions in the 1980s, so too stags "of the teens, twenties, and thirties," write Di Lauro and Rabkin, "displayed narrative and stylistic concerns which almost totally disappeared after the Second World War."[6]

Bereft of almost all concern with story and style, later stags used ugly and old performers. Most of the men appeared to be pimps and the females prostitutes. Performers frequently wore masks or otherwise attempted to conceal their identities by the use of bizarre disguises.

From the 1920s through the 1950s, college fraternities and volunteer social groups like the Elks and Shriners provided the largest market for stag films in America. Patterned after theatrical striptease, stags encouraged male spectators to talk to the projected female image and even to "touch" her spread legs and labia. Unlike later pornos, which seek to satisfy the viewer's sex urge, stags generally aimed to arouse. Brothels used them to encourage potential patrons to buy the sexual favors of their women.

After World War II, the greater availability of projection equipment enabled the stag to move into the home. During the 1950s, they were increasingly shot on 8mm color film, using younger and more attractive performers.

Smart Aleck (1951), the most popular stag ever, starred stripper Candy Barr, then a sixteen-year-old named Juanita Slusher. "I never thought about doing it," Candy Barr told *Oui* magazine in 1976. "But it happened and I've had a lot of flack about it. People say, 'What the hell, it's only a fuck movie.' Well, that was 1951; I do care what the hell. If I had done it by choice, then I would have had some mechanism to adjust it into my lifestyle. But I didn't do it by choice. . . . I wasn't lured. I was taken, done and that was it."[7]

Distinguished only by the youthful presence of Barr, *Smart Aleck*, a typical "motel" film, begins with a traveling salesman inviting Candy into his motel room from the swimming pool. He gets her drunk before making his move. They engage in sex. The only drama occurs when Candy refuses to go down on him. "At the time I wasn't even aware that people engaged in oral sex," she says.[8] To placate him, the fledgling porn star calls in her girlfriend to perform the dirty deed.

Barr's notoriety raises the perennial question of whether such Hollywood stars as Joan Crawford, Greta Garbo, or Marilyn Monroe appeared in stag films. Probably not.

While stag films remained outside the mainstream, nonexplicit exploitation films played on the edge of polite society. "The makers of adult movies, with rare exceptions, are part of a long thriving tradition of American hucksterism," write Eddie Muller and Daniel Faris in their 1996 book, *Grindhouse*.* "From carny barker to holy-rolling evangelist, to grindhouse sleazemeister, the goal has always been the same: promise something extraordinary and then get the hell out of town."[9]

The first mainstream films overflowed with sex. Examples included "exposés" of white slavery like *Traffic in Souls* (1913), orgies (Erich von Stroheim's *The Merry Widow* and *The Wedding March*), and epics that featured Christians lashed at the stake (Cecil B. De Mille's *Sign of the Cross*). Following prohibition of alcohol, however, came prohibition of sex in cinema.

Out of fear of public censure, the studios, then as now owned and operated by secular Jews, chose former Postmaster General Will Hays to create a Production Code Administration (PCA) and act as an internal censor. Irish Catholics Martin Quigley and Joe Breen helped create standards tougher on sex than on violence.

In 1932, Breen wrote to powerful Jesuit priest Wilfrid Parsons about Hollywood Jews.

> They are simply a rotten bunch of vile people with no respect for anything beyond the making of money. Here in Hollywood we have paganism rampant and in its most virulent form. Drunkenness and debauchery are commonplace. Sexual perversion is rampant. Any number of our directors and stars are perverts. These Jews seem to think of nothing but moneymaking and sexual indulgence. The vilest kind of sin is a common indulgence here-

---

*"Grindhouse" refers to an independent movie theater that played sexploitation fare from the 1920s through the early 1970s.

abouts and the men and women who engage in this sort of business are the men and women who decide what the film fare of the nation is to be. They and they alone make the decision. Ninety-five percent of these folks are Jews of an eastern European lineage. They are, probably, the scum of the earth.[10]

Meeting with studio heads, Joseph Scott, a Catholic lawyer hired by Breen and Los Angeles's Bishop Cantwell, described the Jews as "disloyal" Americans, engaged in "a conspiracy to debauch the youth of the land." Scott told the producers that America housed groups "sympathetic with the Nazi assault on Jews in Germany and were even now organizing further to attack the Jew in America."[11]

Founded on Judeo-Christian principles, Joe Breen's Production Code office previewed 98 percent of the movies released in the United States between 1930 and 1968. A first-run house couldn't screen a movie without the PCA seal, and studios wouldn't allow their films to be shown on a double bill with a film that wasn't PCA-approved. Filling this gap were independent producers who displayed all the skin and sin Hollywood couldn't show. These rip-off artists avoided prosecution for obscenity by disguising their movies as cautionary moral tales.

Publicist-turned-pornographer David F. Friedman explains, "The whole secret to the scheme was that the sucker never really saw it all, but, 'Boy didja see that preview for next week's show? We're really gonna see it then.' Of course, they never did. But hope springs eternal in the human breast."[12]

The grindhouse spectacles of the 1920s through the 1950s now seem tame. Expectations exceeded delivery. Producers surrounded the few minutes of illicit behavior—nudity, drugs, sex—with an hour of story. Come full circle, today's "adult" movies concentrate on action rather than story. But in another sense, the more things change, the more they stay the same. Exploitation's grand con of promising something extraordinary and not delivering lives on in X-rated video boxcovers with their glitzy pictures of gorgeous women who rarely appear as beautiful, if they appear at all, in the final product.

Made in Czechoslovakia in 1932, *Ecstasy* ranks as the first sexy art (i.e., nonexplicit) film from Europe. Starring the actress who became known as Hedy Lamarr, the movie created a scandal upon release because of its brief nudity and purple symbolism evoking Hedy's orgasm—rearing stallions, howling winds, and surging flames. An ocean away from American fare, *Ecstasy* depicts a woman who leaves the affluence of her cold, older husband for "ecstasy." Though her estranged husband shoots himself, she's not punished for her sins.

Filmmaker Dwain Esper earned the nickname "King of the Celluloid Gypsies" for creating such exploitation movies as *The Seventh Commandment.* "The whole play is the most thoroughly vile and disgusting motion picture," said Hollywood's censor Joe Breen, "which the three members of this staff . . . have ever seen. It is thoroughly reprehensible . . . offensive and disgusting."[13] Just one of many films of the '30s about venereal disease, *Commandment*, which featured the Caesarian delivery of a dead baby, helped create the genre of sex hygiene.

Though cheap, nasty, brutish, and short (on story), Esper's films always delivered nudity. "Esper created dingy, prurient imagery framed within scripts of fervid moral righteousness. The result was a head-spinning, hellfire-and-brimstone huckster's stew, just like they served at a carnival geek show."[14]

Touring the country with the 1930 classic *Freaks* retitled as *Forbidden Love*, Esper encountered a crowd in North Carolina who threatened to riot when the film didn't deliver. So Esper handed the projectionist a ten-minute reel of frontal male and female nudity and soothed the anger.

While the golden age of burlesque lasted from the mid-1920s to mid-1930s, films of burlesque became popular in the 1940s, though they rarely showed as much skin as a typical MTV video today. Because of different standards of censorship around the country, films starring such performers as Jill St. Cyr and Tempest Storm appeared in as many as three versions, with only the raciest version showing a woman's bare breasts. Jungle pictures, with the simple formula of exotic locations and black nudity, traveled the adults-only circuit for years. Until the 1960s, state censors rarely allowed white women to disrobe.

After World War II, "great numbers of European directors used their artistic and sexual freedom to parlay the zaftig, braless Continental sexpots into fame, fortune, and revolution. Auteur filmmakers such as Michelangelo Antonioni . . . [and] François Truffaut produced a new form of cinema. They could—and did—show nudity, adultery, sex games, rape, foreplay, but never sexual intercourse."[15]

Scandinavian skinny-dipping prepared America for Ingmar Bergman films. *One Summer of Happiness* (1951) tells of a young farm girl's summer of freedom, love, and budding sexuality—all ended by a motorcycle accident. Bergman's 1953 film *Summer with Monika* contained a nude shot of star Harriet Anderson. Fifteen years later, another round of Swedish imports changed the American film industry.

◆◆◆◆

In *Samuel Roth* v. *U.S.* (June 1957), the Supreme Court ruled that for material to be declared legally obscene it had to be "utterly without redeeming social importance." Under this new definition, the U.S. Supreme Court determined that the imported French film *The Game of Love*, which had been closed in Chicago for displaying nudity, was not obscene. The court also quoted *Roth* in overturning subsequent obscenity cases against the homosexual magazine *One* and the nudist magazine *Sunshine & Health*. In 1959, a federal judge, influenced by the new definition of obscenity in *Roth*, rescinded the ban against the novel *Lady Chatterly's Lover*, calling D. H. Lawrence, the book's author, a genius.

Those who pushed America to a more liberal view of sex were mainly male non-Jewish Jews (Jews alienated from Judaism and Jewish life as well as the Christian culture embraced by a majority of Americans) including Samuel Roth of the 1957 Supreme Court case; Grove Press Publisher Barney Rosset; the owner of Olympia Press, Maurice Girodias, and his father, Jack Kahane, a Paris publisher and author of sexually explicit novels; comedian Lenny Bruce; filmmakers Russ Meyer, David Friedman, and Radley Metzger; Austrian psychiatrist Wilhelm Reich; *Screw* publisher Al Goldstein; *Eros* publisher Ralph Ginzberg; publisher Edward Mishkin; Jack Valenti, president of the Motion Picture Association of America; defense lawyer Stanley Fleishman; *Playboy* Playmate and Hugh Hefner's ex-lover Barbara Klein, aka Barbie Benton; Hefner's personal secretary Bobbie Arnstein, philosopher Herbert Marcuse; psychologist Albert Ellis; authors Philip Roth, William Styron, and Norman Mailer; and Supreme Court Justice Abe Fortas. They carried on a hundred year history of radical Jews challenging the reigning order. In the nineteenth century, for instance, most of the madams of major brothels in the Western United States were alienated Jews as were many of the traffickers and prostitutes in the white slave trade.[16] Though only 2 percent of the

American population, Jews dominate porn. Most of the leading male performers through the 1980s had Jewish parents. Leading Jewish pornographers include Wesley Emerson, Paul Fishbein, Lenny Friedlander, Paul Norman, Bobby Hollander, Rubin Gottesman, Hank Weinstein, Fred Hirsch and his children Steve and Marjorie, Steve Orenstein, Theodore Rothstein, and Reuben Sturman.

Born in 1924, Reuben Sturman, the godfather of porn, grew up in Cleveland's East Side, the ambitious eldest son of immigrant Russian Jews who ran a grocery. The future leader of the "Kosher Nostra" served in the Army Air Corps during World War II, then attended Western Reserve University before marrying and starting his own business. Working from home, Reuben drove through Cleveland, visiting candy stores and selling comic books from the trunk of his old Dodge. His business grew by the late 1950s into a wholesale magazine company with warehouses in eight cities.

At the suggestion of an employee, the company began to sell sex magazines and smut paperbacks. Once Sturman realized these items produced twenty times the revenue of comic books, he decided to stock every such publication printed. He eventually produced his own nudie periodicals and opened retail stores. By the end of the 1960s, Sturman ranked at the top of adult magazine distributors.

By the mid 1970s, Rueben owned over 200 adult bookstores supplied by regional distribution companies with regal names such as Royal News in Detroit, Noble News in Baltimore, and the flagship Sovereign News in Cleveland. Though not as well known as *Playboy*'s Hugh Hefner, *Hustler*'s Larry Flynt, and *Penthouse*'s Bob Guccione, Sturman exerted far greater influence. One competitor complained that Sturman did not simply control the adult-entertainment industry; he was the industry.

To guard his privacy, Sturman used at least twenty different aliases, avoided the news media, and frequently hid his face behind a mask during his many court appearances to face such charges as peddling obscenity and tax evasion. "To his defenders in the sex industry Sturman was a marketing genius and a champion of free speech, an entrepreneur whose toughness, intelligence, and boundless self-confidence were responsible for his successes. But to anti-porn activists and Justice Department officials, Sturman was the head of a vast criminal organization whose companies enjoyed an unfair competitive advantage: protection and support from the highest levels of the Cosa Nostra [Mafia]."[17]

In keeping with the *Roth* decision, to avoid prosecution for obscenity, early American filmmakers needed to invent reasons to display the naked human body. So, in 1957, the first nudist colony film, *Garden of Eden*, appeared.

In 1959, three American filmmakers stopped resorting to such inventions as nudist colonies to unabashedly make above-ground movies full of nudity (as opposed to the underground world of fully explicit stags). Russ Meyer's *The Immoral Mr. Teas*, David Friedman's *Adventures of Lucky Pierre*, and Ted Paramore's *Not Tonight, Henry* brought breasts and story to the big screen. Meyer's film was the first, raunchiest, most popular, and most profitable but *Not Tonight, Henry* was the most erotic film of 1955–1960 says porn historian Jim Holliday.[18]

Not Tonight, Henry was the first major film by Ted Paramore, the son of a major Hollywood screenwriter. Paramore began producing erotic loops (ten minutes of film looped in the projector) in 1954. "You were only allowed to shoot girls in bikinis, and then in pasties, then nudes. But you couldn't show pubic hair. These loops were just little stories. No sex."[19]

Starring comedian Hank Henry and narrator Paul Friese, *Not Tonight, Henry* tells the story of a man who, frustrated by his wife, dreams about sex with glamorous figures of history such as Cleopatra, Delilah, Pocahontas, and Lucrezia Borgia. *Henry* illustrates the primary reason for pornography—the human need to fantasize when the real thing either isn't available or isn't satisfying. Generally speaking, at such moments men turn to sexually explicit pictures while women turn to romance novels.

Film director Russ Meyer explored another aspect of the industry: softcore porn. He dominated three decades of soft porn—no penetration or cum shots—specializing in beautifully photographed sex, violence, and big breasts. This Hugh Hefner of adult movies made pictures that together grossed $100 million dollars, four of them ranking among the 1,000 top-grossing films of all time: *Beyond the Valley of the Dolls*, *Vixen*, *Cherry, Harry & Racquel*, and *The Supervixens*. Meyer's 1959 nudie breakthrough *The Immoral Mr. Teas* became the most notorious erotic film released in the United States until 1968's *I Am Curious—Yellow*. *Mr. Teas* set the standard for a new genre of narrative films that featured female nudity and poked fun at the clumsy participants in the game of love.

"There was a vacuum," says Meyer. "The public was waiting for something new. . . . Once *Mr. Teas* caught on, it was booked all over the country."[20]

With 1964's *Lorna*, Meyer moved past nudie-cuties (nudity-filled sex comedies) into realistic drama. Sex now drove behavior. Not love, but lust. "*Lorna* was the first dramatic naked-lady movie," says author William Rotsler. "The films with nudity before then were more vaudeville than drama. . . . Meyer's scripts operated as excuses to create as many opportunities as possible to show female nudity. He wasn't a story-teller."[21] "*Lorna* established the formula that made Meyer rich and famous, the formula of people filmed at top hate, top lust, top heavy. There are few if any subtleties in a Russ Meyer film, any Russ Meyer film. His canvas is vivid, but it is all red or all purple."[22] Meyer peaked with 1968's *Vixen*, the best known and highest grossing of his films. Produced for $72,000, it grossed over $10 million.

Unlike Meyer, whose plot staggered out of the nudity and sex, professional filmmaker Radley Metzger directed feature films whose sex and nudity arose out of the plot. Metzger debuted in 1961 with the softcore *Dark Odyssey*. The second time he filmed, Metzger made a five-minute insert for a French film he'd bought and renamed *The Twilight Girls*. "Some nudity, two girls kissing—I thought the projectionist was going to call the FBI when he ran it the first time."[23] One of the girls in the insert became famous a decade later for her starring role in *The Devil in Miss Jones*—Georgina Spelvin.

David Friedman made the third movie of 1959 to be blatantly sexual: *The Adventures of Lucky Pierre*. Friedman's father, who served as an editor of the conservative *Birmingham News*, owned—along with Friedman's uncle—an amusement park and a chain of movie houses. In 1956, Friedman formed a company to make sexploitation films. He toured the country with a movie that dared to show the birth of a baby—*Mom and Dad*, which he estimates grossed $40 million. Figured in today's dollars, *Mom and Dad* may be the most profitable film ever.

> When I got into the exploitation distribution business in the late '50s, there were four of us in the country—Bill Mishkin and Joe Brenner in New York, myself in Chicago, and Dan Sonney in LA—and the total output in the whole United States was about eight to ten pictures a year, so that the sixty theaters that had to play this stuff every year played each one ten to twelve weeks, gave you a fair percentage, and you made a fortune with it.

> I bought a drive-in in Joliet[, Illinois,] and I had one of the
> first nudie houses in Chicago back when Chicago had a tough
> police censorship board. And it was more profitable than it is
> today when you don't have to submit anything and they're
> playing hardcore in Chicago.[24]

Along with Dan Sonney, the son of Louis Sonney, who
started the exploitation genre in the 1920s, Friedman
bought a run-down theater in Los Angeles that became the
flagship of the Pussycat Theaters. "On the opening day of a
new film you could almost call roll," Friedman remembers.
"The same guys were there, week after week. They'd stand
out front reading the one-sheets [movie posters] so long
you'd think they were studying the Gutenberg Bible."[25]

The adults-only market exploded in the 1960s. Friedman
estimates that at the beginning of the decade there were only
about twenty theaters around the country that showed adult
pictures exclusively. By 1970 that number had jumped to
750. The Pussycat chain built twenty-five theaters from the
ground up to show X-rated movies to supplement the previously existing movie houses they owned. There were forty-
seven Pussycat Theaters in California alone.

"I've exploited the basest human emotions," says
Friedman. "But the one I exploited most was loneliness.
That's who was paying my way, a lot of very lonely men."[26]

Realizing that the nudie-cutie was running out of steam,
David Friedman became one of the first producers to add
violence to sex films. *Blood Feast* appeared in 1963, inspiring
hundreds of imitators. Kenneth Turan and Stephen Zito, in
their book *Sinema*, write

> Unlike the Friedman and Meyer films, which dealt in violence but
> had some artistic merit, the Roughies and Kinkies of the middle
> '60s generally represent the nadir of the sex-exploitation film, ugly
> in spirit and appealing to the worst instincts of humankind.

The death rattle of the woman with the severed leg replaces the unfettered cry of ecstasy, and blood rather than semen becomes the symbolic fluid of erotic expression. Paradoxically, these grotesque films, featuring neither complete nudity nor loving sexual contact, were largely exempt from the wrath of the censors, possibly because the United States has traditionally been a country that censors sex but tolerates violence.[27]

The husband and wife team of Michael and Roberta Findlay created numerous cinematic crimes against humanity. Under the name Anna Riva, Roberta began performing in sex films before moving behind the camera with Michael to make 1965's *Satan's Bed*, which features the rape of a mute Yoko Ono. Next came their "Flesh" trilogy—*Touch of Her Flesh*, *Curse of Her Flesh*, and *Kiss of Her Flesh*, which displayed various methods of murdering nude women such as a poisoned cat's claw dragged across a naked midriff, electrically charged earrings, and razor-studded dildos.

(In a case of life imitating art, Michael Findlay himself came to a grizzly end. Headed for Europe in 1974 to seek investors for his invention of a portable 3-D camera, Findlay was decapitated by the propeller of a helicopter that crashed into the roof of the Pan Am building in Manhattan.[28])

As one long hooked on the sexually sadistic side of cinema, pornographer Bill Margold wrote

there is nothing more arousing than sexual terror. A helpless woman being strangled, stabbed, axed, suffocated or drowned is the most exciting thing I can watch. It unlocks my fantasies.

Nineteen seventy-one must be remembered for a slickly sick slice of sexual sinematics called *The Psycho Lover*. . . . This show had it all. A nut goes about strangling and stabbing women and the police are baffled. Each of the murders is done with care for the viewer's arousal. He [the murderer] uses the strangulation method combined with sexual taunting and terrorism. A stylish dual electrocution/execution at the end of the film (with much writhing about) was particularly stimulating.[29]

Margold makes explicit the dark desires of many men for
achieving the ultimate revenge against women—murder. In a
less dramatic fashion, standard porn reveals the male desire
for revenge through its habitual depiction of facial cum shots.
Just as there are few jokes without a victim, so, too, there is
little porn without a victim.

The nasty films of the 1960s and 1970s made by Friedman and company show that without some form of restraint,
either industry-imposed or government-imposed, pornographers gleefully churn out a product that drips with blood as
well as semen.

The year 1966 was a particularly bad year for literature—the
two runaway best sellers were *Valley of the Dolls* by Jacqueline
Susann and *The Adventurers* by Harold Robbins. In the
spring, *New York Times* literary critic Lew Nichols wrote,
"Seldom has there been so wretched a collection of titles as
appears today."[30] And in June a journalist thought up the literary hoax *Naked Came the Stranger*.

"The act of conception [of the hoax]," recalls *Newsday*
columnist Mike McGrady, "took place, fittingly, in a gin mill.
Fittingly—because the gin mills that year were filled with
writers anesthetizing themselves against the harsh new reali-
ties of their profession. To be a serious writer in the 1966 was
also to be, by inclination if not by definition, a serious
drinker."[31]

On a Tuesday night, McGrady sat drinking at a gin mill
known unofficially by its largely journalistic clientele as "the
bureau." He felt depressed as he recalled his recent interview
with Harold Robbins and his attempt to read *Valley of the
Dolls*. As McGrady found solace in alcohol and male com-

panionship, he had an epiphany and turned to a couple of fellow reporters. "Why don't we all do one? A novel. Everyone could do one chapter and each would write about one specific perversion . . ."[32]

Twenty-five *Newsday* employees, mainly journalists, each wrote sections of the sex-drenched novel that became *Naked Came the Stranger*, which describes in pornographic detail the adventures of a wife who seeks sexual satisfaction through sex with loads of men. (McGrady cast as author Penelope Ashe, a demure suburban housewife who resembled Jacqueline Susann.)

Seeking a publisher, McGrady visited the office of Lyle Stuart, who specialized in trash. Poster-sized photographs of the communist revolutionary Che Guevara grabbed McGrady's attention as he entered the office, as did two large cardboard cartons filled with books and carefully labeled "Sex Soft" and "Sex Hard."

"It's not just that Lyle Stuart and Che Guevara were friends," remembers McGrady, "which they were. But Lyle Stuart is to the publishing world what Che Guevara was to the world of international diplomacy."[33]

Well into their first meeting, McGrady told Stuart about his prank—a bunch of journalists getting together to write a truly bad book.

"I'll publish it," Stuart said.

"It should be ready in a year or so," McGrady replied. "You can read it then."

"I mean I'll publish it sight unseen," was the response.

"You mean without reading it?"

"Of course."

That was Lyle Stuart's way. He generally refused to read books that he published. "That may seem strange to someone who is new to book publishing," says McGrady, "but the remarkable thing is that so many publishers do read what they publish."[34]

In 1969, *Naked Came the Stranger* exploded like an orgasm to the top of the *New York Times* bestseller list, helped along initially by *Screw* magazine and later by exposure of the hoax in *Time*, *Newsweek*, the *New York Times*, the *Los Angeles Times*, and the *Washington Post*. A year later, McGrady published a book about the experience titled *Stranger Than Naked or How to Write Dirty Books for Fun & Profit*.

In 1980, ten years later, McGrady and Stuart conspired on another hoax that largely remains undiscovered: a book that profiled a leading star of the fledgling porno industry—Linda Lovelace.[35]

The first legitimate film to show pubic hair, Michelangelo Antonioni's *Blow Up*, appeared in 1966, followed a year later by the laborious *I Am Curious—Yellow*, which overflowed with full frontal nudity. Underground, stags became known as loops and producers shot increasingly in color. (Although the first color feature films were released in 1939, porn was shot in black and white until the 1950s.) Body painting flicks proliferated as an excuse for showing skin. "Then came the beaver shorts ["beaver" is slang for vagina], the split beaver shorts and features that dealt with S&M, spankings, whippings and the like," writes porn historian Jim Holliday. "By the late sixties, color feature films showed full body simulation. This was only a step away from IT."[36]

Sexually explicit material remained outside popular culture until the 1960s, when notions of sin, shame, and guilt diminished. Literature, plays, and movies became raunchier and sex shops, adult movie houses, and strip joints proliferated. After dropping its production code in favor of a ratings system in 1968, Hollywood unleashed such experimental fare as *Easy Rider, Bonnie and Clyde*, and *Midnight Cowboy*.

During the turbulent 1960s, which lasted in spirit through most of the 1970s, the nation's ethic, says social scientist James Q. Wilson, changed from self-control to self-expression.[37] It became okay to do your own thing. Along with drugs and rock'n'roll came porno chic.

"To deny sex is to deny life," writes William Rotsler. "To reject art is to impoverish yourself, rejecting pleasure and growth. To accept sex and art together is to add to oneself, to be positive instead of negative. Erotic cinema . . . reveals us to ourselves with increasing artistry. . . . Perhaps it will be the catalyst that finally breaks us loose, as a culture, from centuries of ugly repression."[38]

Many leftists supported pornography because it subverted middle-class morality. Sexually explicit movies brought into the open the most private act that was supposed to occur only in the bedrooms of married couples. Porn equalizes human beings. "Sex strips away identities it takes a lifetime to build," writes John Hubner. "A naked aroused man is not a brain surgeon or a university president or a Methodist bishop. He is an animal with an erection."[39]

"Sex is the one area that is innately subversive to the rules and regulations of society, and pornography is the celebration of the subversive side of sex," says Dr. Martin Blinder, a San Francisco psychiatrist who testified in dozens of obscenity cases. "Pornography revels in all of sex's deliberately subversive permutations. It shows sex in a convent or a schoolroom, all the most unlikely places. We all have fantasies about our ninth-grade English teacher, and in pornography you can subvert her dignity. There she is with her butt in the air, getting it in both holes."[40]

The late psychiatrist Dr. Robert Stoller offered a more sober perspective on "free love": "Humans are not a very loving species, especially when they make love. . . . Harm energizes erotics. . . . The desire to harm, cruelty, anger, revenge, and humiliation is the grain of sand around which the pearl of erotic excitement exists."[41]

Notes

1. *Encyclopedia of Crime and Justice*, Vol. 3 (New York: Free Press, Macmillan, 1983), p. 1077.

2. Al Di Lauro and Gerald Rabkin, *Dirty Movies* (New York and London: Chelsea House, 1976), p. 10.

3. Ibid., p. 11.

4. William Rotsler, *Contemporary Erotic Cinema* (New York: Ballantine Books, 1973), pp. 28–29.

5. Ibid., p. 21.

6. Di Lauro and Rabkin, *Dirty Movies*, p. 27.

7. "Smart Aleck Candy Barr," *Oui* (April 1976): 75.

8. Ibid.

9. Daniel Faris and Eddie Muller, *Grindhouse* (New York: St. Martin's Press, 1996), p. 9.

10. James R. Peterson, "A History of Sex in the 1930s," *Playboy* (August 1997): 146.

11. Ibid.

12. Faris and Muller, *Grindhouse*, p. 17.

13. Ibid., p. 21.

14. Ibid., p. 22.

15. Rotsler, *Contemporary Erotic Cinema*, p. 32.

16. See Dennis Prager and Joseph Telushkin, *Why the Jews: The Reason for Antisemitism* (New York: Simon & Schuster,

1983), pp. 59–70; and Paul Johnson, *A History of the Jews* (New York: HarperCollins, 1988), pp. 655–57.

17. Eric Schlosser, "The Business of Pornography," *U.S. News & World Report* (February 10, 1997): 51.

18. Jim Holliday, *Only the Best* (Van Nuys, Calif.: Cal Vista Direct Ltd., 1986), p. 192.

19. Personal interview with Ted Paramore, April 11, 1996.

20. Faris and Muller, *Grindhouse*, pp. 82–83.

21. Rotsler, *Contemporary Erotic Cinema*, p. 35.

22. Ibid.

23. Jay Kent Lorenz, "The Erotic World of Radley Metzger," *Psychotronic Video*, issue 17 (Winter 1994).

24. Faris and Muller, *Grindhouse*, p. 135.

25. Ibid.

26. Ibid., p. 136.

27. Kenneth Turan and Stephen F. Zito, *Sinema* (New York: Praeger Publishers, 1974), p. 25.

28. Faris and Muller, *Grindhouse*, p. 105.

29. Bill Margold, "Sex and Violence," *Hollywood Press* (October 1975): 34.

30. Mike McGrady, *Stranger Than Naked or How to Write Dirty Books for Fun & Profit* (New York: Lyle Stuart, 1970), p. 6.

31. Ibid.

32. Ibid., p. 9.

33. Ibid., p. 81.

34. Ibid., p. 84.

35. Linda Lovelace with Mike McGrady, *Ordeal* (New York: Lyle Stuart, 1980).

36. Holliday, *Only the Best*, p. 17.

37. James Q. Wilson and Richard Hernstein, *Crime and Human Nature* (New York: Simon & Schuster, 1985).

38. Rotsler, *Contemporary Erotic Cinema*, p. 15.

39. John Hubner, *Bottom Feeders* (New York: Doubleday, 1992), p. 62.

40. Ibid.

41. Robert Stoller, *Sexual Excitement: The Dymanics of Erotic Life* (New York: Pantheon Books, 1979), p. 53.

2

Deep Throat

*M*odern porn arose in the early 1960s in the seedy streets of Soho, London, with the mass production and international sale of such quality black-and-white loops as *Pussy Galore*, *First Audition*, *End of Term*, and *100% Lust*. "Our kind of porn really started in Soho, not in Sweden or Denmark as many believe," says veteran German pornographer Hans Moser. "Denmark was just the only liberated country in Europe which would take it. Walter Bartkowski was the main distributor for 'the Gentlemen of Soho' and he handled slides, picture sets and 8mm black-and-white films."[1]

Bartkowski was a German Polish prisoner during World War II who decided to stay in Britain after the cessation of fighting. Using the name Charlie Brown, he became London's top porn smuggler by the late 1950s while working as a steward on the boats carrying passengers from the British Isles to Scandinavia.

Smuggled into the United States and Europe in the thousands, British porn films of the 1960s stressed kinky behavior such as sadomasochism and anal sex. Several of pornographer Mike Freeman's loops came to the attention of Italian Alberto Ferro on a trip to London in 1966.

The prodigal son of a diplomat, Ferro started peddling porno (copies of Hugh Hefner's nude calendar photograph of Marilyn Monroe) at his Swiss high school in 1954. He entered the Sorbonne in 1955 and fell under the sway of Camus' philosophy of pleasure. In late September 1961, a newspaper headline caught his attention: "International Gang of Pornographers Arrested in Genoa." One of the young men arrested had the same surname as Ferro's girlfriend, who lived in Milan. Ferro called her. In tears, she said that the man arrested was her older brother Dino. Ferro suggested to Dino's lawyer, who was inexperienced in matters of "obscenity," a line of defense that Ferro was researching for his doctorate in law thesis at Milan State University: Representation of licit sex cannot be considered illicit.[2]

Quitting law school, Ferro devoted himself to smuggling porn. Able to speak five languages, Ferro drove through customs with impunity because of his Diplomatic Corps license plates. With demand for porn films increasing, he traveled to London in 1966 and bought some clumsy 8mm loops from Mike Freeman's Climax Film productions. After almost getting arrested at the Alpine railway tunnel between France and Italy, Ferro retired from smuggling and devoted himself to production of color porn loops, believing that production of quality erotica would bring eventual legalization. In 1967, Ferro inspired a young Danish member of parliament of the Social-Democratic Party to sponsor legislation that decriminalized sexually explicit books and pictures. Denmark's decision made news around the world, especially when government statistics showed a decrease in sex crimes the year after the abolition.

Ferro began his first loop, *Golden Butterfly*, starring himself and his girlfriend, in June 1967, and by a year later had completed four more—*Chains, Suzi la Blonde, Blow-Up 69*, and *Sex on the Motorway*. Deciding against selling the rights to his product to Freeman, Ferro set up his own production and marketing company, AB BETA, in Stockholm. To avoid trouble with the police network Interpol, in 1970 he borrowed the name and papers of his Swedish carpenter, Lasse Braun.[3] Under his new moniker, Ferro made loops about Caribbean performers, prostitutes, Casanova, Vikings, and anal sex. Simple and mechanical, this technically proficient Northern European product was the best of its kind, featuring beautiful though blasé performers, prototypes of 1990s Vivid Girls. On one of his trips to Sweden, Ferro met the enthusiastic Brigitte Maier, the young American porn starlet and *Penthouse* covergirl. A few months later, she moved in with Ferro and his wife as a permanent houseguest and eventually became the star of his first feature films.

In 1970, Ferro received a call from excited American distributor Reuben Sturman, who'd just seen double penetration (a woman simultaneously penetrated by two men, one vaginally and one anally) for the first time in the Lasse Braun film *Delphi in Greece*. Sturman eventually bought fifty loops. "The deal was incredible," remembers Ferro. "Over the next four years, they made a million copies of each one of them. This was before Caballero [a production company] even got started. For all those years, the top thirty or so short films were my films." Used in Sturman's peep shows across the United States, the ten- minute loops probably grossed over two billion dollars.[4]

Sturman also spent millions with the Theander brothers of Denmark. Born during World War II, Peter and Jens Theander opened a magazine shop in downtown Copenhagen in

1966 and eventually cornered the Danish hardcore market until legalization in 1969. The brothers then founded Candy Film, which became the world's biggest producer of Super 8mm film. As their production exceeded the capacity of local processing plants, the Theanders created a huge porn production camp on the outskirts of Copenhagen in 1975. Over the next two decades, the brothers produced nearly 100 million magazines, 9 million Super 8's, and over 1 million videocassettes.[5]

Technological advances fueled porn production during the 1960s. Photolithographic color-printing machines, which reduced costs while increasing picture quality, allowed Scandinavian publishers to introduce the first widely available color photos of vaginal, anal, and oral penetration. Over the next two decades, Europe published over 250 billion sexually explicit pornography magazines.

Europe's most powerful pornographer, however, was Germany's Beate Uhse. In 1962, she opened in Flensburg what many regard as the world's first sex shop, selling sex toys as well as pornography. Soon she developed similar operations in every major German city. When West Germany legalized hardcore in 1975 but prohibited mail order, Uhse's profits soared.

The porn revolution left no part of the Western world untouched, not even the rural northern California town of Antioch, where future pornographers Jim and Artie Mitchell grew up.

In his superb book on the Mitchell brothers, *Bottom Feeders*, journalist John Hubner points out that like mainstream films, porn reflects the society that produces it. Most Westerns, for instance, feature a scene where a John Wayne–type wraps his arms around a feisty young lady and tries to kiss her. The young lady beats his chest with her fists and struggles to break free. Then she melts, closes her eyes, and passionately returns the kiss. Porn, then, now, and probably forever, is that scene over and over again. Only instead of a kiss, the girl ends up submitting to sex.

Expanding on this analogy, Hubner says that pornography is an adolescent male daydream. Boy meets girl; girl fulfills boy's every desire. Life isn't like that (and therein lies porn's appeal), particularly in a conservative town like Antioch. But in *The Nun*, a black-and-white 8mm stag film made in about 1950 that was probably the Mitchells' introduction to cinematic sex, things happen the way young men wish they happened. In the film, a woman dressed as a nun walks into a room and a Peeping Tom watches as she undresses. He finally enters the room. She resists, but like the leading ladies in the old John Wayne films, eventually submits.[6]

For years, journalists repeated the myth that the brothers turned to each other while watching *The Nun* and said, "Hey, bub. An ole boy could make himself a lot of money with these movies." Supposedly, in that moment, their careers in porn were born. In fact, neither Jim nor Artie had a clue what they were going to do after high school. Jim studied film at San Francisco State University and in 1968 he began shooting stills and later 16mm moving pictures of naked women. He worked nights in a porn theater, seeing how much money trash brought in. He figured that if lonely men huddled in back rooms paid to watch grainy, blurry, simulated scenes of intercourse shot in hotels, they'd spend much more to watch professionally filmed real sex in comfortable surroundings.

During these revolutionary times, the personal, including the sexual, became political. Through porn, the Mitchell brothers made money and revolution, love and war. "The outsider-outlaw feeling was much alive in Jim and Artie," says psychiatrist Dr. Martin Blinder. "Their bent may have sprung from the same anti-authoritarian, sociopathic drive that formed Bonnie and Clyde."[7]

Inseparable, Jim and Artie seemed more like identical twins than just brothers, never staying in the same room together for longer than a few minutes without going over and dropping a hand on the other's shoulder. In temperament they differed—Artie was friendly and outgoing while Jim appeared serious and subdued. Neither tolerated criticism of the other behind his back for each held loyalty as his supreme value.[8]

On July 4, 1969, the Mitchell brothers opened the O'Farrell theater and began showing "beaver" films—endless reels of women masturbating with their fingers or pulling their labia apart to reveal huge on-screen vulvas and deep vaginal tunnels.

"If the cops hadn't bothered us," says Jim Mitchell, "we probably wouldn't have gotten into stories. The purest form of titillation is the single girl auto-masturbation film . . . and the beaver film was a truer form for getting off on some auto-erotic fantasy. When it opened up and you added fucking, you had to show the man and you covered up the girl. . . . It disrupted the auto-erotic trend of sex films. It was boring because all anyone wanted to see was the close-up penetration shots."[9]

The Mitchells' main competition were Alex deRenzy's Screening Room and Lowell Pickett's Sutter Cinema. Pickett, an aging beatnik, tried to eliminate the external cum shots, but people stopped showing his films because while they were funnier and more dramatically developed, they violated pornographic convention. As Jim Mitchell often said, "The only Art in this business is my brother."[10]

Early pornographers like the Mitchells, Pickett, and deRenzy often owned theaters, thus by-passing distributors.

Frequently bankrupt small businessmen, they came from every background except film.

By early 1969, San Francisco hosted two dozen theaters showing beaver films and few people protested aside from Diane Feinstein, then a candidate for the San Francisco Board of Supervisors and leader of a band of antiporn crusaders. "What distinguishes San Francisco from any place else is the style with which porn is marketed, its practitioners' attitude toward it and the tolerance most square citizens display concerning the whole question," wrote the *New York Times Magazine* in a January 1971 article called "The Porn Capital of America." "The flourishing underground press in San Francisco all share the idea that porn, even at its sleaziest and most bizarre, is an important and healthily revolutionary ingredient of the new culture."[11]

Adult theaters arose all over America and their owners sought San Francisco porn. "We'd shoot two versions, a hard-core for here and a soft core for elsewhere," remembers Pickett. "The places we shipped hard-core versions always surprised me—San Diego, Indianapolis, and small towns all over the country where, I presume, the authorities were being paid off."[12]

Public concern over pornography led to a presidential commission which included Nixon appointee Charles Keating, the founder of Citizens for Decent Literature. After spending $2 million and two years in research, the 1970 Report of the Presidential Commission on Obscenity and Pornography found little evidence that porn caused harm. The commission recommended that the United States follow Denmark's lead in abolishing censorship of sexually explicit materials.

Furious with the majority report, Keating, along with Father Morton Hill and several other commissioners, alerted the White House to the moral damage the report could cause the country. Richard Nixon rejected the majority's recommendations. He pointed out that a Democratic president (Lyndon Johnson) had appointed the commission and that the Democrats were as soft on porn as they were on communism.

Until 1957, U.S. law governing obscenity patterned itself after the *Hicklin* decision in England in 1868, which said that a book could be banned if as much as one paragraph on one page was deemed to be lewd. But in a majority decision of the U.S. Supreme Court written by Justice William J. Brennan in 1957, obscenity came to be defined as material "utterly without redeeming social importance." The Mitchell brothers' 1971 conviction (which was later overturned) for showing obscene films that had no plots led to an important evolution in porn. To give their explicit films "redeeming social importance," the Mitchells and other pornographers began adding stories. Jim and Artie pioneered the featurette (short feature film) and the pornographic feature film, pumping out 336 before *Behind the Green Door* was released. Easier to defend in court, the films drew more varied audiences than the single lonely men who watched loops.

Documentary films then broke through the hardcore feature barrier. In 1968, Alex deRenzy and a partner traveled to Copenhagen to film Denmark's first sex fair and in 1969 they released the first feature film showing sexual intercourse, *Censorship in Denmark*. Made for $15,000, the documentary grossed $25,000 the first week on its way to an eventual box office of over $2 million. Numerous competitors soon followed suit with feature-length films done in a pseudo-documentary style thought to be immune from prosecution for obscenity. In 1970, Los Angeles's John Lamb made *Sexual Freedom in Denmark*. In New York, Gerard Damiano made *Sex U.S.A.*, starring future porn stars Linda Lovelace and Harry Reems, and *This Film Is All About....* Alex deRenzy gathered classic stags into *A History of the Blue Movie* followed by Bill Osco's inferior *Hollywood Blue*. The first advertised porn feature in the major New York newspapers, Mike Henderson's *Electro Sex '75*, appeared on Labor Day weekend 1970. Freddy Hanson made *Animal Lover in Denmark*, featuring farm girl Bodille doing a dog, pig, and horse. Matt Cimber, the husband of Jayne Mansfield, made *Man and Wife*, the first 35mm porn film to get national distribution.

Bill Osco, part of the Osco drugstore chain family, promoted the first classic porn feature: 1970's *Mona the Virgin Nymph*, made by his friend Howard Ziehm. *Mona* displays dramatic structure and credible relationships with the actors developing their characters through dialogue. Unlike the documentaries, this film uses a story: A virgin named Fifi develops her oral sex skills under her father's instruction. Pornographic in intention and execution, *Mona*, which appears on *Variety*'s list of the top fifty grossing films of 1971, follows the classic pattern of erotic scenes from dalliance to sadistic orgy. The movie features many of porn's themes: seduction, incest, a permissive-seductive parent figure, dirty words, nymphomania, lesbianism, masturbation, orgies, oral sex, bondage, sadomasochism, and sex toys.

Soon other adult theaters in San Francisco followed the Mitchells' lead and storylines became more common. Lowell Pickett's films tried to be both erotic and artistic. In an artistic rut and financial hole, pioneer Alex deRenzy poured out pseudo-documentaries, trying to recreate the success of *Censorship in Denmark*.

❖❖❖❖

Director Gerard Damiano created two of porn's most famous names, Linda Lovelace and Harry Reems, through his 1972 feature *Deep Throat*. More than a quarter century later, Linda Lovelace remains porn's best known star. Her third published autobiography, 1980's *Ordeal*, sold out several print runs. Just as *Deep Throat* remains porn's best selling movie, *Ordeal* remains the best selling book on porn. While *Throat* shows porn as harmless fun, *Ordeal* shows porn as vicious. The two perspectives reflect the dominant reactions to porn.

In 1986, Linda published her fourth book about herself—*Out of Bondage*. Together with *Ordeal*, these two books (written by Mike McGrady and initially published by Lyle Stuart, the pair who perpetrated the 1969 literary hoax, *Naked Came the Stranger*) shape public perception of the adult film industry as exploiters of vulnerable women. This view developed not so much from the contents of the books, but from what millions of people believe—due to sensational media coverage—the books describe.

As she received more and more attention during the 1980s, Linda expanded on the horrible things she claimed she suffered as a sex object. Appearing on TV shows and in media interviews, Linda Lovelace–turned–Linda Marciano elaborated upon the degradation described in her books. For example, in an interview with the *Toronto Sun* published March 20, 1981, she claimed such things as that a gun was held to her head during the filming of *Deep Throat* to make her perform the disgusting tricks that are portrayed. A careful reading of *Ordeal*, however, taken on face value, reveals a woman suffering from domestic abuse and finding relief only on occasion, such as when she performed sex on camera.

Chuck Traynor, who was married to Linda during the early 1970s, is portrayed as a villain by Lovelace in her last three autobiographies. He confirms the basic truth of the events described in *Ordeal*, but denies Lovelace's claim of being a victim. Along with virtually every person who knew the couple in the early 1970s, including Gerard Damiano and Harry Reems, Chuck says Linda willingly participated in *Deep Throat*, porno loops, rough sex, and prostitution.[13]

Lovelace became an archetype for what journalist Hart Williams calls the "Linda Syndrome"—porn stars who seek acceptance from "overground" society by disavowing their porn past.[14]

Born Linda Boreman in 1950, Lovelace was the daughter of a New York policeman. She grew up in Yonkers, attending Catholic schools such as St. John the Baptist in Yonkers and Maria Regina High School in Hartsdale. The ordeal that was her life began early. "When I was four years old, [my mother] started beating me—first with a belt, later with the buckle of the belt." One day Boreman brought home the wrong kind of nosedrops and got slammed with a broomstick for the mistake. Her mother told her that she would've gotten the right bottle if she didn't have her mind on boys so much.[15]

During grade school Lovelace wanted to become a nun. Few guys dated her more than once, she says, because she wouldn't put out. She earned the nickname Miss Holy Holy. "I was the type of girl who liked to go down to the ocean and hold hands," recalls Linda. "I still am."[16]

She lost her virginity when she was nineteen and the next year she gave birth to an illegitimate child that her mother forced her to put up for adoption.[17] Lovelace lived in New York City until a car accident wrecked her life and body. A skidding Chrysler hit her car, smashing her face into the windshield, breaking her jaw and several ribs and lacerating her liver. She moved to Florida to live with her parents during her recuperation. One hot Florida day in the summer of 1967, Linda met Chuck Traynor. After a few weeks she moved in with him and began turning tricks. The couple moved to New York in 1969, where the Happy Hooker,

Xaviera Hollander, turned down Lovelace as a potential employee.[18]

At the same time, struggling actor Rob Everett picked up *Screw* magazine and answered an ad looking for sex performers. Over the next few months the unhappily married young man posed nude for several magazines, and eventually received a call from Linda's loop director, Ted Snyder.

"Do you think you can get it up?" Snyder asked Everett. The insecure blond answered yes and he received directions to a loft near Broadway. The place had unmopped floors, a filthy sink, and odd pieces of furniture covered by sheets, and it stank. "The people who made filthy movies," says Lovelace, "always seemed to live in filth."[19]

Everett arrived to find Snyder, the director and cameraman; Chuck Traynor; and his partner for his debut porn performance—Linda. She found Everett adorable and their first shoot went smoothly.

"There was no sound [recorded] and no lunch," remembers Everett. "Linda was nice. She enjoyed working with me. She loved sex. . . . No guns were held to her head to make her perform. She loved what she did. Linda is the one person responsible for keeping me in porn because she constantly called me to perform with her," says Everett, who later took on the porn name Eric Edwards.[20]

Lovelace and Edwards did two dozen loops together. Edwards usually earned $40 and Lovelace $50. "I thought that it was unfair that the guy got paid less than the girl seeing that he does all the work. I still think that's unfair."[21]

Edwards lived in an unhappy marriage with a woman he had met while they both attended the American Academy of the Arts. Sexually incompatible, they became swingers. "I was young and not into that sort of thing, but I found that other women were into me. My wife would also have her own experiences. The situation made me feel like a man. I was pleasing women and they enjoyed being with me."[22]

Doggarama, a loop illegal to sell in the United States and another of Lovelace's porno blockbusters, shows Edwards and Lovelace indulging in anal sex before the blond stud leaves. Appearing unsatisfied, Lovelace looks around and sees a dog. She snaps her fingers and says "Ooooh."

Norman, the dog, pads over and Lovelace starts sucking his dick.

"I was floored," says Edwards, who earned only half as much as the dog's owner.

> After I finished doing Linda, I just sat back and watched. She was really into it. I was in awe. I had never seen a woman with a dog before, but it became the thing to do.
>
> It was a strange period. There were no real laws then. The business was going any which way it could. There were stud dogs and there were losers. We'd have a strange dog come onto the set to do actress A and he wouldn't like her and he wouldn't get into it. So the actress would try placing a hot dog in her pussy and covering it with mayonnaise. But this dog was a stud. He knew what to do. He mounted [Lovelace] from behind and did her doggie style. I don't know why they didn't bring any cute girl dogs for me.[23]

In *Ordeal*, Linda claimed that she was threatened with a gun and told to perform sex on the dog or die.[24] Porn historian Jim Holliday contradicts her, however.

> I talked to the five people who made *Doggarama*. Eric Edwards, Chuck Traynor, the cameraman-director [Bob Wolf], the dog's owner, and the money man. Their story is the same. I'm going to take the word of a woman [Linda Lovelace] with an axe to grind over five persons who were there? Let the public think what they want. I'm telling you, she's full of it. These five guys to conspire and tell a story and remember it for many years . . . that would be a conspiracy that would make me want to have them installed as the directors of the CIA. . . .

> The owner of the dog says that Linda, a couple of days after, asked if the dog was still available.[25]

Lovelace gained a reputation for her enthusiasm for fucking dogs. She reportedly put on bestiality shows for Hugh Hefner and company at his Playboy mansion in West Los Angeles.[26]

Director Gerard Damiano discovered Lovelace in one of her 8mm loops. He owned one-third of Gerard Damiano Film Productions. With money from his father, Anthony, Louis "Butchie" Peraino owned the other two-thirds of the company. Under Damiano's direction, Lovelace starred with Harry Reems in an 8mm cheapie, *Sex U.S.A.*, the first movie produced by the Peraino-Damiano partnership.

One day while driving from his apartment to his Manhattan office, Damiano had a vision. Traynor and Lovelace sat waiting in his office when he arrived.

"We're going to do a film about a girl who has her clit in her throat," said Damiano. "Linda will be perfect for it. The most amazing thing about Linda is that she still looks sweet and innocent."[27]

Butchie didn't agree, however. He wanted a big-breasted blonde like Carol Connors. Afraid of losing Lovelace's $1,200 salary for the film, Traynor talked Peraino into allowing Lovelace to blow him. She sucked him off daily and kept the starring role.[28]

Butchie's dad, Anthony, bankrolled the movie for $22,000. In his sixties, Anthony drove down to Florida, when the film was being shot, with Lovelace and Traynor. The cast and crew—a soundman named Norman, cameraman Harry Flecks, Harry the gaffer, and a couple of others—stayed at the Voyager Inn on Biscayne Boulevard in Miami while filming the most profitable movie of all time.

Though Lovelace claims Traynor beat her savagely on the first night of the shoot and that the crew heard her screams, no one else on *Deep Throat* remembers such an occurrence.

Deep Throat begins with Linda complaining that she's never had a bell-ringing orgasm. She visits Dr. Young (Harry Reems). After determining that her problem is not caused by childhood trauma, Dr. Young guesses that her problem is physical. An examination proves him right; Linda's clitoris is in her throat. He tells her that the solution is to relax her muscles and take a penis "all the way down." Linda tries fellatio with Dr. Young, taking the entire length of his penis into her mouth and finally achieving the sexual pleasure she's been longing for. Grateful, Linda offers to marry him and be his slave. Dr. Young rejects her offer because his blonde nurse, Carol Connors, wouldn't like it, but he offers Linda a job making house calls.

Deep Throat opened to the raincoat* crowd in June 1972 at the New World Theater on 49th Street in New York City. Over the next few months, millions of Americans for the first time watched explicit sex. According to Turan and Zito, in their book *Sinema*, Frank Sinatra, Spiro Agnew, Warren Beatty, Truman Capote, Nora Ephron, and Bob Woodward (who used "Deepthroat" as the name for his key Watergate source) took in the film on its first run, and eventually more people saw *Deep Throat* in theaters than any other porno.[19]

Deep Throat brought hardcore into popular culture, earning at least twice as much money as any other porno in history. *Deep Throat* played for eight consecutive years at a theater in Hollywood until replaced by *Exhausted*. Accurate earnings are impossible to come by in porn because it is not

---

*According to the stereotype, raincoaters are men who arrive at adult theaters wearing raincoats to allow easy access to their genitals while fantasizing about the women on screen.

in the interest of distributors to release dollar figures of sales and rentals, even if they are known. Most business is conducted in cash to avoid taxes in particular and the government eye in general.

In 1987, David Friedman said that *Deep Throat* grossed at least $100 million theatrically.

> I know that Pussycat paid the Peraino brothers [the distributors of *Deep Throat*] $3 million in film rentals. Those figures are good because Pussycat is a legitimate operation—they paid checks. And that $3 million was only for showing the picture for about a year in one cinema and about six years at another.
>
> I would say that the total amount of film rental paid to the Perainos was somewhere in the neighborhood of $35 million. If an established distributor had handled the film, it would have been more like $50–$60 million. Now, 60% rental translates down to 40% after publicity and distribution costs. The net figure is about 40%, so *Deep Throat* must have taken at least $100 million at the box office by now. That excludes video.[30]

Whatever the exact box office, the flick made for $22,000 over six shooting days in Miami became the most profitable film ever and inspired thousands of imitators.

"The porn film scene of 1973 is strikingly reminiscent of Hollywood during that pioneer era when making any sort of movie was considered disreputable," wrote *Playboy* movie critic Bruce Williamson, "when actors, writers, and directors cranked out primitive two-reelers under assumed names, lest their colleagues in legitimate theater or publishing circles accuse them of prostitution."[31]

Deep Throat and *The Devil in Miss Jones* ranked among the top ten grossing films of 1973, encouraging the *New York Times* to coin the phrase "porno chic" to describe the growing fascination with sex on film. Mainstream critics initially ignored and then panned *Deep Throat* as both film and eroticism, though Al Goldstein, editor of *Screw* magazine, called it "the best porno ever made."[32]

Reviewed by major New York film critics, *Deep Throat* eventually received unprecedented recognition for a porno movie, attracting "a whole new audience of seemingly regular folks who were willing to pay $5 each to see oral sex performed on a 40 foot screen," wrote the *Los Angeles Times*. "For acts once considered unspeakable, Linda Lovelace became a national celebrity—deemed suitable for the talk show circuit and slavered after by some Hollywood deal makers."[33]

Director Gerard Damiano admits *Deep Throat* was a joke. As a movie, it's average. Why then all the hype from mainstream reviewers? Holliday says the critics cheered for explicit sex far superior to the loops they may have seen on the side. "They went ga-ga over routine filmmaking and opened the door for public acceptability."[34]

"One of the things I liked best about the film," says Bill Rotsler, "was Linda's obvious delight in what she was doing. It was infectious and made the entire film more palatable. . . . Right now the language of porno cinema is baby talk—but inevitably some of it will become poetry."[35]

In its eighth month in New York, *Deep Throat* kept drawing crowds. *Variety* for January 10, 1973, reported,

> Grosses at the World Theater continue in record-breaking proportions . . . but the real impact is measured not so much by the spinning turnstiles as by the types of folks being introduced to the theatrical hard-core fare. A visit to the World [Theater] on Friday revealed the house fully sold out for a mid-afternoon show and a line outside composed of elegant unaccompanied ladies, young couples, middle-aged couples, and at least three silver-haired matrons with shopping bags who looked like refugees from Schrafft's.[36]

Not all critics liked *Deep Throat*. Ellen Willis wrote in the *New York Review of Books* that she found the porno "witless, exploitative, and about as erotic as a tonsillectomy."[37] Nora Ephron wrote in *Esquire* that the film was "unpleasant, disturbing. . . . Not just anti-female but anti-sex. . . . I came out of the theater a quivering fanatic. Give me the goriest Peckinpah any day."[38]

A legally embattled movie, *Deep Throat*'s first major trial ranged over eleven days in New York near Christmas 1972 and attracted worldwide attention. Expert testimony came to more than one thousand pages of trial transcripts, and the opinions expressed regarding the film varied widely.

Film historian Arthur Knight: "I found in *Deep Throat* an attractiveness about the people. . . . A real attempt to use humor in depicting sex."[39]

Sociologist Ernest van den Haag: "The presentation of sex, divorced from emotional relationships . . . as an act of mutual exploitation . . . permits the personalities of the participants to be totally disregarded. . . . They are . . . bearers of sexual organs and not human beings who are ends in themselves. I not only regard it as being without redeeming social value; I regard it as highly antisocial."[40]

Professor of medical psychology Dr. John Money: "It [the movie] indicates that women have a right to a sex life of their own, and they are not simply an instrumentality of men's sex life which is the way things used to be. . . . There is a theme in the film which implies that women should get sexual satisfaction and sexual gratification."[41]

Judge Joel E. Tyler decided that the experts had not shown that 51 percent of the movie had redeeming social value and fined the theater $3 million. He wrote that *Deep Throat* was "a feast of carrion and squalor . . . a Sodom and Gomorrah gone wild before the fire . . . one throat that deserves to be cut . . . a nadir of decadence. . . . It does, in fact, demean and pervert the sexual experience, and insults it, shamelessly, without tenderness and without understanding of its role as a concomitant of the human condition."[42] Says Tyler, now retired, "If I were to make that decision today, I would be deemed a fool."[43]

Bob Sumner described the ruling on his New World Theater marquee while he booked a new film: "JUDGE CUTS THROAT, WORLD MOURNS."[44]

Deep Throat arrived after the sexual revolution peaked and fewer real girls were easy. Men frustrated by reality could now turn to X-rated movies and find flesh for fantasy, vivid images on a silver screen of beautiful women sucking and fucking. Sucking was particularly a treat as fewer nice girls gave head in the world before *Deep Throat*.

"Most people who watch porn fear and mistrust women," Jim Holliday told psychiatrist Robert Stoller.

By sheer lack of personality they've become subjugated to the women in their lives. If I was going to write a book, a cute title would be 'What Porn is all about: Blowjobs and Losers.' The blow job is the one thing the average American guy wants from his woman, but she won't give it to him. So he seeks release in a porno.

At the extremes are people who fear and hate women, who will never be able to relate to women in real life. But they are not the threat who go out and do the damage. The Pussycat theaters have a fantastic slogan that I'm surprised the anti-porn forces haven't capitalized on. It's like, "For those who never knew and for those who will never forget." Does that not smack of losers and old guys?[45]

While *Deep Throat* did not originate the "money shot"— sperm ejaculated all over a woman, particularly her face—it gave millions their first sight of it—again and again. Though the initial purpose was to prove that the sex on film was real,

pornographer Bill Margold says that the money shot repre-
sents vicarious male revenge on women. "Every man has
wanted someone he couldn't have. So he harbors revenge.
When we come on a woman's face or brutalize her sexually,
we're getting even for the man's lost dreams."[46]

Deep Throat popularized the money shot and many other
conventions of adult films. New age nudist Robert Rimmer,
who wrote sexually utopian novels such as *The Harrad
Experiment*, summarizes porn cliches in the *X-Rated Videotape Guide*:

- Men rarely ejaculate inside the women, rather they
  come on their breasts, lips, or stomach while they
  climax. Women love sperm showered on them, it tastes
  good to the last drop.
- Women love sucking cock and usually initiate it. They
  can deepthroat a foot of dick for several minutes
  without gagging.
- Up until 1978 women and men didn't talk much, and
  certainly didn't say "I love you." Rather, "It was a
  great fuck."
- After a few licks of her vagina, the man usually sticks
  his dick into her. She's lubricated and on the verge of
  an earth-shattering orgasm because she so enjoyed
  sucking his cock.
- Afterplay is even rarer than foreplay.
- Emotions—even love, fear, and jealousy—are rare.
- Most sex vids have one lesbian scene.
- Most males are circumcised—John Holmes is the big
  exception.
- Most 1970s sex vids begin with a class ambiance and
  story that equals Hollywood productions, but usually
  the story gets lost after fifteen minutes.

- Relationships are rare.
- Most females since the early '80s have breast implants which you can tell by their perkiness when the women are standing, lying, or being touched.
- Many adult films cater to a male fantasy of having a virgin who learns all she knows from him.[47]

Writer Lynn Snowden adds these conventions:

One. The characters' names are the same as their own noms de porn. One supposes this is done to avoid confusion among particularly dimwitted fans. Two. Whenever a character is alone in a room, he or she masturbates. If someone else comes in, the two characters have sex. If another person comes in, they too join in.

No one ever expresses indignation or surprise—they simply hurry out of their pants, since the action, rather than the plot, must be constantly moving. No one delivers flowers, reads the meter, or even looks out the window without engaging in intercourse.[48]

Susie Bright notes that even the background music has its conventions. "The history of the porn soundtrack has gone from Mantovani rip-offs to aerobic disco to something that sounds like a cheap version of the soundtrack from *The Piano*. I hate them all, but I can't bring myself to push MUTE because I might miss any yummy groaning and gasping."[49]

Immediately following the *Deep Throat* breakthrough, the release of *Last Tango in Paris* shook the cinema world. "This is a breakthrough precisely because it is not a porno film," notes Rotsler, "but does put into graphic visual form an erotic relationship which includes anal rape. It is a milestone film not so much for its eroticism, which is debatable, but because an Oscar-winning major star [Marlon Brando] chose to make it, and make it at a time he was in contention for another Oscar, which he won and rejected."[50]

Last Tango in Paris plays a significant role in the history of erotic cinema because it demonstrated increasing public acceptance of erotic cinema.

Now pop culture celebrities because of the success of *Deep Throat*, Lovelace and Traynor flew to Los Angeles where Lovelace posed for a *Playboy* pictorial. They visited Hugh Hefner at his Playboy mansion. Hugh said he loved *Deep Throat* because it was more than straight sex, but also had comedy and a story.

Eager to cash in on the Linda Lovelace phenomenon, pornographers stuck together various loops of Linda to form such awful movies as *The Confessions of Linda Lovelace* and *Linda Lovelace Meets Miss Jones*. Lovelace also appeared in several loops that featured her urinating and absorbing a fist and a foot into her vagina. Linda became the best-selling author of *Inside Linda Lovelace*. Every night for two weeks, she received a list of questions to answer on a tape recorder. The publisher added nude pictures of Lovelace to the transcription of her answers and created a best seller. The book's message appeared in the opening chapter. "I live for sex, will never get enough of it, and will continue to try every day to tune my physical mechanism to finer perfection."[51]

During 1973, Linda filmed a sequel to *Deep Throat* directed by Joe Sarno that received a limited softcore release amid the confusion following the Supreme Court's *Miller* ruling on obscenity, which will be discussed later. Dining at a Malibu restaurant with *Playboy* movie critic Bruce Williamson, Lovelace said, "*Throat II* will be a backward step if they take out the hardcore. I don't want to back away. I'm not looking for a big Hollywood career. I'm a porno star. I just want to be Linda Lovelace."[52]

Just before Christmas 1973, Linda appeared in the play *Pajama Tops* at the Locust Theater in Philadelphia but the show bombed. On January 31, 1974, Lovelace was arrested in the Dunes Hotel in Las Vegas for illegal possession of cocaine and amphetamines.[53]

"After *Deep Throat*, the business simply passed Linda by," says Eric Edwards. "She wasn't particularly attractive nor could she act. If she'd told the truth about her life her book may not have sold as well as making up a story that claims she was forced to do these disgusting things."[54]

Lovelace eventually left Chuck Traynor for producer and choreographer David Winters. They developed two nonexplicit projects, both awful: the movie *Linda Lovelace for President* and the book *The Intimate Diary of Linda Lovelace*. Neither condemns porn, for Linda at this point had yet to be "born again."

A heavy drug user through the 1970s, frequently combining marijuana with Percodan, a painkiller, Lovelace eventually split from David Winters and married plasterer Larry Marciano, with whom she had two children.[55]

Lovelace became friendly with Gloria Steinem, who introduced her to other feminists. The *Deep Throat* star then found Jesus and experienced an epiphany. All that fucking and sucking in her past had been forced on her. She hated it. She was a victim. She wasn't responsible for her behavior. Evil pornographers forced her to do disgusting tricks at the point of a gun.[56]

"When you see the movie *Deep Throat*, you are watching me being raped," Linda told the *Toronto Sun*. "It is a crime that movie is still showing; there was a gun to my head the entire time."[57]

Unable to find mainstream acting work, Lovelace and her new family lived off welfare until she published *Ordeal* in 1980 and *Out of Bondage* in 1986. Afforded generous media coverage, she became the most frequently offered example of porn's exploitation of women.

Amid Lovelace's notoriety, it's easy to forget the few qualities that made her famous: "The fresh carnality, the air of thoroughly debauched innocence, the sense of a woman exploring the limits of sexual expression and feeling. Linda Lovelace is the girl next door grown up into a shameless . . . woman."[58]

In 1973, prior to her "conversion," Lovelace told *Variety*: "I'm not going to sit here and say I'll never do another hard-core film because I was forced into this one, that I needed the money. . . . I did it because I loved it. It was something I believed in. And if, when I'm sixty-five years old, they're making an X-rated movie and they need a little old lady to be in it, I'm gonna say, hey, I'm right here."[59]

Though a one-shot wonder, Linda Lovelace became the most famous porn star by giving American men what they wanted most—blowjobs.

❖❖❖❖

While Lovelace quit porn in 1974, her *Deep Throat* co-star Harry Reems worked through the late 1980s. Reems earned thousands of dollars distributing *Deep Throat*, but he landed in a Memphis jail in 1975 charged with conspiracy to distribute obscenity. Jack Nicholson and Warren Beatty raised money for his defense. Initially convicted, the decision against Reems was overturned two years later on appeal led by Harvard law professor Alan Dershowitz.[60]

Reems retired from porn in 1976 but returned in 1982 when Reuben Sturman funded his $75,000 salary, probably the most money ever paid to a person to do a porno. Reems screws twelve women in the film *Society Affairs*. The shooting went days over schedule because Harry couldn't get his penis erect on camera.[61]

Between jobs, Reems spent the 1980s bouncing in and out of detox centers, mental institutions, and jail, chased by tax problems, bad debts, and outstanding arrest warrants. He hit bottom in 1985, when he slept behind a grocery store dumpster in Malibu. He had a two-quart-a-day vodka habit. Bill Margold saved his life one night by pulling him out of the gutter on Sunset Boulevard.[62]

After five days in a Los Angeles jail in 1989, and another arrest in Park City, Utah, Reems sought help in a twelve-step program "I knew if I didn't stop," Harry told *People* magazine, "I'd die."[63]

In 1984 in Park City, Reems had met Jeanne Sterrett, a pretty redheaded waitress. After eleven months of sobriety, Reems called her, and on their first date, he proposed. Before she accepted, Sterrett watched *Deep Throat* with friends. It's a movie still banned in Utah—a porn-free state. "I thought it was hilarious," says Jeanne. "I loved it, but I didn't think it was the Harry I knew."[64]

A trustee of his church, Reems now sells real estate. Unlike his *Deep Throat* co-star, he no longer talks about his porn past.

Notes

1. David Hebditch and Nick Anning, *Porn Gold* (London: Faber & Faber, 1988), p. 212.

2. Ibid., p. 198.

3. Ibid., p. 202.

4. Ibid., p. 204.

5. John Heidenry, *What Wild Ecstasy: The Rise and Fall of the Sexual Revolution* (New York: Simon & Schuster, 1997), p. 57.

6. John Hubner, *Bottom Feeders* (New York: Doubleday, 1992), p. 35.

7. Ibid., p. 62.

8. Ibid., pp. 186–87.

9. Robert Rimmer, *The X-Rated Videotape Guide* (Amherst, N.Y.: Prometheus Books, 1993), p. 27.

10. Hubner, *Bottom Feeders*, p. 136.

11. Quoted in ibid., p. 81.

12. Ibid., p. 111.

13. Ibid., pp. 237–41.

14. Personal interviews with Hart Williams, May 1997.

15. Linda Lovelace with Mike McGrady, *Ordeal* (New York: Lyle Stuart, 1980), p. 5.

16. Ibid., p. 7.

17. Ibid.

18. Ibid., p. 97.

19. Ibid., p. 101.

20. Personal interview with Eric Edwards, May 31, 1996.

21. Ibid.

22. Ibid.

23. Ibid.

24. Lovelace, *Ordeal*, p. 105.

25. Interview with Jim Holliday, April 18, 1996.

26. Lovelace, *Ordeal*, p. 207.

27. Ibid., p. 117.

28. Ibid., pp. 120–22.

29. Kenneth Turan and Stephen F. Zito, *Sinema* (New York: Praeger Publishers, 1974), p. 143.

30. Hebditch and Anning, *Porn Gold*, p. 194.

31. Bruce Williamson, "Deep Throat," *Playboy* (October 1973): 115.

32. Quoted by Linda Williams, *Hardcore* (Berkeley: University of California Press, 1989), p. 74.

33. Ellen Farley and William K. Knoedelseder Jr., "The Pornbrokers," *Los Angeles Times*, June 13, 1982.

34. Jim Holliday, *Only the Best* (Van Nuys, Calif.: Cal Vista Direct, Ltd., 1986), p. 23.

35. William Rotsler, *Contemporary Erotic Cinema* (New York: Ballantine Books, 1973), p. 14.

36. Quoted by Farley and Knoedelseder, "The Pornbrokers."

37. Quoted by Turan and Zito, *Sinema*, p. 143.

38. Ibid.

39. Ibid., p. 144.

40. Ibid., pp. 144–45.

41. Ibid., p. 145.

42. Quoted in ibid., p. 145.

43. Benjamin Svetsky, "Oral Argument," *Entertainment Weekly* (February 26, 1993): 68.

44. Turan and Zito, *Sinema*, p. 143.

45. Robert Stoller, *Porn* (New Haven, Conn.: Yale University Press, 1991), p. 167.

46. Ibid., p. 31.

47. Rimmer, *X-Rated Videotape Guide*, pp. 27–29.

48. Lynn Snowden, "A Prude's Guide to Erotica," *Cosmopolitan* (May 1993): 83–84.

49. Susie Bright, "The Prince of Porn," *Playboy* (August 1994): 42.

50. Rotsler, *Contemporary Erotic Cinema*, p. 39.

51. Lovelace, *Ordeal*, p. 210.

52. Williamson, "Deep Throat."

53. Turan and Zito, *Sinema*, p. 148.

54. Edwards interview.

55. Turan and Zito, *Sinema*, p. 148, and Lovelace, *Ordeal*, p. 172.

56. Linda Lovelace, *Out of Bondage* (New York: Berkley Books, 1986), pp. 3–8.

57. "Linda Lovelace's Ordeal," *Toronto Sun*, March 20, 1981.

58. Turan and Zito, *Sinema*, p. 148.

59. Ibid.

60. Farley and Knoedelseder, "The Pornbrokers."

61. Luke Ford, "Harry Reems," posted at http://www.lukeford.com/b75.html (July 1997).

62. Steve Dougherty and Dirk Mathison, "Born Again Porn Star," *People* (May 13, 1991): 83.

63. Ibid.

64. Ibid.

3.

The Devil Behind the Green Door

*T*he success of *Deep Throat* stunned its maker, Gerard Damiano. "It keeps knocking me on the head every time I turn around. Being recognized in public places, my phone never stops ringing. . . . I'm the one who believes it least."[1]

Born in 1929, the hard-working high school graduate never collected an unemployment check. In the mid-1960s, Damiano owned a couple of beauty salons in Queens. Through his accountant, who worked for an independent low-budget filmmaker, Damiano entered the film industry. He started by working for nothing, then moved up to grip, production manager, cameraman, and finally, after three years paying his dues, director.

Damiano took the usual route from soft- to hardcore by making *Marriage Manual*, *Changes*, and *Sex U.S.A.* in the fake documentary style then immune to obscenity prosecution. "Six months after *I Am Curious—Yellow*, we came out with *Marriage Manual*, the first time we did real sex. But there was always a doctor telling you this could help your marriage. In *Sex U.S.A.*, too, we gave them the old socially redeeming values. By the time of *Deep Throat*, I had decided to do what I liked. How can you convince people that what you are doing is legit, if you don't believe in it yourself?"[2]

In 1971, Damiano decided porn needed to lighten up. The result was *Deep Throat*. "I created a monster, because all of a sudden there's a lot of people cranking out sex pictures, making money with crap, making money without ever having paused to learn the craft."[3] Unlike most of porn's leading directors, Damiano never made any films released to a general audience. MGM president Jim Aubrey brought Damiano in to talk to studio executives in 1971 but they couldn't agree on a project. In 1973 Damiano made a mainstream film that was never released.

After *Deep Throat*, Damiano produced and directed 1972's *The Devil in Miss Jones* (*DMJ*), the fourth highest grossing porn film ever. "*Throat* is a joke," says Damiano. "*Miss Jones* is a film."

The X-rated industry's first attempt to make an art movie, according to Bill Margold, *The Devil in Miss Jones*'s structure of sex scenes—oral, straight, anal, lesbian, masturbation, three-way, kink, and double penetration—set the industry standard.[4] The 1974 book *Sinema* declared *DMJ* the best erotic film ever made and most critics place it on their all-time top ten list. *DMJ*'s sole creator, Damiano worked as the producer, director, cinematographer, editor, and distributor through his own company, MB Productions.

The movie begins with a scene reminiscent of Jean-Paul Sartre's *No Exit*. In her New York City apartment, virgin spinster Justine Jones (Georgina Spelvin*) commits suicide

---

*A tradition in the theater assigns the name "George Spelvin" to any actor who doesn't want his real name known or who is playing a part so small that credit would be an embarrassment. Hence, the name of *DMJ*'s lead actress, "Georgina Spelvin" was an inside joke.

from guilt over her lustful thoughts. Before going to hell, Justine, who takes her name from the protagonist of the Marquis de Sade novel of the same name, experiences the lust that she never acted out in life. Five minutes into the film, Miss Jones meets her teacher, Harry Reems, who seeks to cure her inhibitions by placing a dildo in her ass. Harry threatens to punish her if it falls out.

She performs fellatio and says, "I love the taste of it. Please, I want to know what it feels like in my cunt," so they have sex. Justine's fruitless pursuit of orgasm seems the logical extension of sex without personal commitment. The only quality that Justine values in any man is the hardness of his cock. Miss Jones reverses the traditional stereotypes by presenting a woman who uses men solely as a means of sexual gratification.[5]

Damiano believed in *Miss Jones.*

> It's always a shock, even to me, seeing hardcore blown up twenty times bigger than life, so I thought of doing it softcore, then decided hell, no, the time had come for a good pornographic art film. I hoped audiences were ready to take us seriously if we stopped making fun of our sexual problems. Why can't we just look at sex as sex, and not think we've always got to make people laugh to justify it? The movies have been masculine fantasies up to now, exploiting women because you played to the male audience. But the audience today includes women, and I consider *Miss Jones* a totally feminine film. It's the males who become meat, reduced to objects of her fantasy. And it's the penis she's in love with, not the man.[6]

To put it simply, Justine, *DMJ*'s only fleshed-out character, reduces men to their cocks. While Damiano and critics described it as a "feminine" film, *DMJ* simply varies the male daydream: Most men would love to be "used" by women for sex.

Born in 1936, the future Miss Spelvin first performed in

a USO show in San Antonio at age five. Spelvin wanted to be an opera singer but her voice wasn't good enough. Her second choice was ballerina. After that it was a series of compromises. She played the lead in the 1966 original production of the Rodgers and Hammerstein musical *The Pajama Game*. Five years later she danced briefly in *Hello Dolly*. Despite her apparent success, Spelvin was an alcoholic. Broke and with her career on the skids, Spelvin accepted an offer to do *The Devil in Miss Jones*.[7] Over the next ten years, she appeared in one hundred adult movies.

Even in her prime, Georgina, 5'4", 120 pounds, and 36-25-36, appeared more plain than beautiful: "I'm slightly cross-eyed and my head is too big for my body." But she was an excellent actress. "My face changes. No one feature is accentuated. I can make my face emphasize whatever quality I want, from one role to another, and it does what I want."[8]

Both broke and drunk in New York in 1972, the future Georgina Spelvin had a film in post-production. She saw ads for actresses wanted for "sexploitation films." Spelvin made appointments with producers, and carrying her resume and portfolio, she gave them this pitch: "I know I'm probably not what you're looking for in the way of an actress. Yet, if you need someone to help carry cable, run sound, hold a boom, carry lights . . ."[9]

About the third man she saw listened to her with amusement and offered work. Because he wanted to shoot on a boat, Spelvin found one for him, and supplied friends for some of the acting parts. Spelvin played a madam.

> It was softcore, low budget, low quality, but it paid the rent for a month. I got friendly with one of the grips, and he called me a month later and asked me if I wanted to act in a sex picture he was making called *Parental Guidance*. This was to be hardcore, and he wanted to know how I felt about sex in front of the

camera. Fornication was the word he used—would I fornicate for the camera? I told him it would depend on who my partner was. I'd have to meet the man before I could decide. Well, I met the leading man and he was nice, attractive and we got along fine. So I took the job.[10]

While making the picture, Spelvin met stud Marc Stevens, who introduced her to Harry Reems. He told her that Gerry Damiano was making a film on location that weekend and they needed a cook. They got one.

In the middle of figuring out her menu, Spelvin was interrupted by Reems, who asked if, as the only woman on the set, she'd read some scripts.

I did the most ordinary job of reading the woman's lines while they tried out the men, but from the comments I got you'd think I was Helen Hayes in an Oscar role. They raved about me. The infant X-rated industry had never been exposed to a woman who had any theatrical background or training. So to these people, I was a great actress.

They rewrote the script to make the heroine, Miss Jones, not a 19-year old buxom sexpot, but a 36-year-old, flatchested old maid. It worked.[11]

The Devil in Miss Jones wasn't released for nearly a year after it was shot, and during that time Spelvin did numerous one-day wonders. "I was having a ball. I was never a nympho, but I've always liked sex. So fornicating for the camera didn't bother me. I exercised choice of partners. I had to like the man to some degree. I was at the peak of my sexuality, about 35 or 36, and I had no qualms about capering around in front of the camera. I was a professional actress, and I was doing a job that I was good at."[12]

While making porn films, Spelvin kept working stage and straight movies. "The two worlds are so different. If people want to put me down for acting in porn, they have to admit they've seen a porn picture. A few people outside the industry know about my 'other career,' but I think they secretly admire me. Now and then someone will whisper with a leer 'Made any good pictures lately, Georgina?' "[13]

As of 1996, Spelvin worked as a computer production designer to pay the mortgage on her modest home. She says porn has its place, but not in the public square.

❖❖❖❖

With its serious, depressing tone, *The Devil in Miss Jones* symbolized New York porn, which had more in common with decadent European productions than those of the West Coast. In turn, American features of porn's Golden Age (1972–1983) frequently had more in common with European products of today and yesterday than it does with 1990s American porn. Since the beginning of cinema, sex on screen has appeared more dramatic and self-conscious in America than in Europe. For example, Hedy Lamarr's 1932 film, *Ecstasy*, shocked U.S. audiences with its nudity, sex, and lack of punishment for the adulterous heroine.

Characteristics that unite America's best porn features of the 1970s with Europe's best of the 1990s include thought, experimentation, comparatively high production values, and raunch. "The Europeans take a longer time to get to the point," says Californian Bill Margold, "but it's prettier. We make movies in a motel room. They do it in a museum."[14]

Not only are European flicks "prettier," they are also nastier. Depending on the country, European productions have long shown anything from bestiality to "golden showers" (urinating on someone) to bondage videos featuring explicit sex. These examples of decadence appeared in American productions of the 1970s but ceased by the early 1980s.

With few exceptions, American filmmakers have yet to produce the sophistication of European sex romps such as *Emmanuelle* and *Bordello*, both released in 1974. Nudity and sex appear to be more serious matters in America, in large part because of its religiosity, regarding sex as holy rather than just another biological function.

American porn veteran Porsche Lynn articulates the secular and more European perspective: "Everybody needs to come. Sex is a biological need. It's not an immoral disgusting thing. Sex is like drinking water and eating food. And just as you need to breathe air, you need to have sex."[15]

Southern California became the leading producer of pornography by the mid-1970s, just ahead of New York and San Francisco. What distinguished Los Angeles from the competition were its beautiful women and its lack of concern for plots, politics, and pretense. Los Angeles specialized in loops and New York in features while San Francisco produced equal amounts of both.

In many ways, San Francisco related to Los Angeles during the 1970s the way Europe related to America. The older northern city has always been more sexually liberal. In the 1960s, San Francisco enjoyed topless bars while Los Angeles worried about bikinis. San Franciscans saw beaver loops when Los Angelenos saw only bare breasts. And while San Francisco police made the occasional bust, they lacked the vindictiveness of Los Angeles cops.

The schlock came from Los Angeles though the city had numerous filmmakers willing to make hardcore. San Franciscans shot more frequently on location while their southern counterparts, afraid of the police, shot behind closed doors. "We're less afraid to try things up here," a San Franciscan told William Rotsler in the early 1970s. "In Hollywood they have the Big Studio thing that mucks everything up."[16] Cinematographer Tony Haze worked both cities. "San Francisco movies have a *cinema verité* quality. They go places, they get out of four walls, they do things, and they get the hell out of the bedroom. In Los Angeles moving the screwing from the bedroom to the shower is considered going on location."[17]

San Franciscans seem more interested in making statements, Los Angelenos in making profits. Politics in the northern city are more radical. The counties beside the two cities, Marin County in the north and Orange County in the south, rank among the wealthiest counties in the United States but their politics contrast—Marin is liberal, Orange conservative.

Part of the difference between the two approaches may come from the geography—Los Angeles is flat, sunny, and suburban while the San Francisco Bay Area is colder, hillier, and more varied.

Los Angeles eventually won the production battle, however, and the San Fernando Valley now makes 90 percent of America's porn. During the 1990s, the San Francisco–Los Angeles divide between professionalism and enthusiasm developed into a mainly L.A. amateur versus feature competition.

"These strip-malled, sun-baked, single-storied San Fernando Valley communities are where Southern Californian dreams go to die," writes journalist Karl Taro Greenfield in the September 30, 1995, *A.* magazine.

> The per capita income in the Valley is lower than on the upscale West Side of Los Angeles, as is the likelihood that a resident holds a college degree; the chance a child will grow up in a two-parent household; and . . . the price of real estate. About the only things higher in the Valley than on the West Side are the temperature and the death rate.
>
> The formula is as concise and brutal as the Pythagorean Theorem; broken hopes minus options adds up to a career in . . . "adult" video. White girls. Black girls. Asian girls. Girls of every

background who dreamed the California fantasy, came here to find it, and failed. Where dreams die, porn thrives.

Born April 22, 1952, Marilyn Briggs, porn's biggest star of all time, "dreamed the California fantasy." She fled her loveless home in 1969 to model in New York. She did topless stills, Pepsi and Clairol commercials, and the movie *The Owl and the Pussycat*, in which she appears in bed half-naked. When Barbra Streisand, who also appeared in the film, didn't want to tour to promote it, the job fell to Briggs. She later moved to Los Angeles where an important producer offered her a deal: He'd provide her with an apartment, car, acting lessons, spending money, roles in major films, and career guidance in exchange for Briggs being his mistress. Not wanting to be tied down to an old man with a big paunch, she rejected his offer. On his way out the door, the shocked producer told Briggs that she'd never make it in the biz. He was right. Briggs never succeeded in mainstream entertainment.[18]

Finding no work in Los Angeles in 1971, Briggs moved to San Francisco but still could not find acting jobs that paid. The slim blonde danced nude for a few weeks but quit because it depressed her. While working as a waitress in a health restaurant, Briggs read an ad placed by the Mitchell brothers about a major film they were casting. She rushed to the O'Farrell Theater and read the audition notice which asked if the actor wanted a balling or non-balling part. Briggs at first thought the notice meant bowling but in a few minutes she realized that the film was X-rated. She turned to leave.

It had been a depressing day for Jim and Artie Mitchell— all the girls who'd answered their ad appeared burned out. Then they saw the fresh-looking Briggs leave the building.

Jim and Artie chased after her and by late that afternoon they'd signed her to do their movie. When Briggs told her beatnik husband she had a part in a porno he became angry, but Briggs stood by her decision.

The Mitchells gave Marilyn the last name "Chambers" to go with her starring role. The youngest of three children, Marilyn had spent her life unsuccessfully competing for her parents' attention. Learning that she couldn't please them, she decided to defy them. By appearing in *Behind the Green Door*, writes John Hubner, Chambers got to defy and impress her family in a way they'd never forget.

So that her reaction to being raped would be genuine, Chambers never read the script of *Behind the Green Door*, which is based on an anonymous story that men had been passing around since World War II. "That's why I think the film hit," says Chambers. "I lost my inhibitions onscreen at the same time Americans everywhere were losing theirs."[19]

According to John Hubner, in his book *Bottom Feeders*, Chambers, nineteen years old, smoked a joint of marijuana to calm herself before the filming began. She plays Gloria, a woman who is kidnapped from a hotel and taken to a secret sex club. Former All-Pro defensive end with the Oakland Raiders, Ben Davidson plays the bouncer at the club and the Mitchell brothers play Marilyn's kidnappers. Six women dressed in black robes—the weird sisters—take Marilyn on the club's stage, remove her clothing, and play with her body. Then out strides the ex-boxer Johnny Keyes painted like a savage. He performs endless cunnilingus on an anguished Chambers, who looks around like she hopes that everything will soon be over. It won't.

Keyes eases up her body and inserts his penis into her vagina. He strokes long and hard, in and out, as Chambers winces with pain. As she thrashes about, Keyes follows her eyes, insisting that she recognize him. Finally she surrenders, wraps an arm around Keyes, and kisses him. Keyes rides on until he and Chambers appear to simultaneously orgasm.

Next, five men in white tights with the crotches cut out mount the stage. Three men get on trapezes and another lies down on the floor. The weird sisters bring Marilyn out and guide her onto the penis of the man lying down. The three men on trapezes lower themselves to Chambers, and she takes the middle man's cock into her mouth. She shudders, then begins masturbating the other two men on the trapezes. The fifth man tries to suck on her breasts while the women in black fondle her.

Chambers masturbates the men harder as the audience— a group of about a dozen people watching the show—starts screwing each other. The men on stage ejaculate all over her. The end result is a complex ten minute scene with advanced special effects. "The image of one of the men ejaculating into the heroine's mouth is shot in extreme slow motion," write the authors of *Sinema*, "and it is repeated and reworked by dissolves, overprinting and reverse printing. The color is solarized, and the image becomes brilliant, abstract, and changeable. Chambers' elegant characterization of a victimized woman is achieved without a single line of dialogue as she moves with conviction from terrorized, passive virginity to willing sexual maturity."[20]

Eventually, George McDonald rushes on stage to rescue Chambers and they run away to his van to make love.

"The movie was made under conditions so hot," says Artie Mitchell, "we just wanted to throw down the camera at the end of each of day of filming and fuck and suck our way to oblivion."[21]

Based upon the male fantasy of kidnapping a beautiful woman and forcing her to do everything you want, *Green*

Door could not be made today—the theme of rape is no longer acceptable fare.

On opening night at the O'Farrell, George McDonald felt too nervous to go inside the theater to watch. He stayed outside and awaited reactions. As the movie ended, guests came out thrilled but confused. On the biggest night of McDonald's life, the projection man had mixed up reels two and three. "Only in porn could that happen and the audience still enjoy what they saw," reflected McDonald.[22]

Even shown in sequence, *Green Door* makes little sense. A crucial fifteen minutes of film burned up in the developing lab. The 16mm film is grainy, blurred at times, and the sound, as usual in a Mitchell brothers production, inept. But despite the technical problems, *Behind the Green Door*, shot for a total investment of $60,000, earned about $50 million, making it the second highest grossing porn movie ever.[23]

When Marilyn's parents found out about it, they refused to talk to her for years.

In 1973, the justices of the New York Supreme Court ruled that four films, including *Green Door*, contained so many "acts of sexual perversion, [they] would have been considered obscene by the community standards of Sodom and Gomorrah." In response, the Mitchells spent almost a million dollars to make the 1975 bomb *Sodom and Gomorrah*, probably the most expensive porno ever. The *San Francisco Chronicle*, the first daily newspaper to regularly review porn, found the movie "as dull as watching a pile drive on a construction site. . . . It is an abysmally shoddy spectacle of sex and violence that is . . . without humor, imagination or production values, a skimpy, painfully witless, dunderheaded retelling of the story of Lot and his daughters in Sodom."[24]

◆◆◆◆

Born in 1945, blond, ageless wonder "Eric Edwards" appears in 1,000 pornos, the only person to perform sex on film in the 1960s, '70s, '80s and '90s.

One of sixteen winners out of 24,000 entrants, Edwards received a two-year scholarship from ABC-TV to attend the American Academy of Dramatic Arts in New York. For his audition, Edwards played a part from *The Taming of the Shrew*, a role he's never mastered in real life.

After graduating from the academy in 1967 and receiving his diploma from the hand of actress Helen Hayes, Edwards signed with the William Morris Talent Agency. Over the next eight years, he performed regularly on stage at summer stock programs around the country and appeared in commercials for Gillette, Coleco Toys, and Close Up toothpaste. Needing money, he posed nude for several magazines and began performing in sex loops with Linda Lovelace. His wife sometimes joined them. If Edwards hadn't been away at summer stock, he probably would have appeared in *Deep Throat*. Its success produced a demand for people who could act and perform sex. Edwards's commercial for Close Up toothpaste was taken off the air when the company found out about his other "acting."

Edwards did his first blue movie (sex flick) for director Chuck Vincent in 1973—the R-rated *Blue Summer*. Edwards went X in *Slip Up*, made shortly after *Deep Throat*, a time when most porn features were burlesque sequences with explicit sex. Golden Age productions most resembled musicals, only the characters soared into sex rather than song.

"When they first started putting legal pressure on this industry," remembers Edwards, "the public thought we were being run by the Mafia. But for the most part, this business has always been run by Jews. Just normal businessmen . . . smart guys who know how to make a buck."[25]

Edwards did many movies in San Francisco for Gary Graver, aka Robert McCallum.

> It was such a joy to hop on a flight all paid for, have a drink, come down, have a limo waiting for you, and deliver you to your hotel suite, and get handed your script. Everything was so finely organized. Being an actor, I didn't know anything about the production end, but I knew we were trying to do something of quality. It was like regular movie making. Bring the talent in, put them in a hotel, take care of them, give them a food budget, bring them on to an organized set. . . . Those were the good old days. . . .
>
> Gerry Damiano and I share a vision of making high quality, big budget erotic films. I was impressed by his wanting to make a good product. My favorite movie of his was *Memories within Miss Aggie* because it gave me the opportunity to act. Back in the '70s and early '80s, they were all trying to make bigger and better products. They wanted to enhance the business by making more than a sex movie. But then the government put rules and regulations on us. We were in an uphill climb to make a good product. We'd have gala openings. I printed my hands and feet in cement on Pussycat Theater in Santa Monica. There were Kleig lights, limos. . . . Those were the glory days.[26]

During the industry's "glory days" (1976–1985), Edwards earned up to $1,000 a day. In a May 31, 1996, interview, he explains that the average male porn star then earned $500 a day and the actor would typically work several days on a film. "You didn't have sex three times a day like now. Maybe I'd have one sex scene in the entire movie but I'd have five days of dialogue."

Despite his high earnings, Edwards has "no concept" of how much money he actually made. He admits that much of his paycheck went up his nose in the form of cocaine. The porn star blames his addiction on first great love—sex performer Arcadia Lake, whom he met in the late 1970s.[27]

Edwards struggled through the early 1980s with his

cocaine problem. He was smart enough to refuse work when he was strung out on drugs. Edwards was good friends with porn legend Harry Reems, who was an alcoholic. "Harry would call me and say he was on a street corner someplace and he didn't know where he was. He wanted rescue. This awakened me, too."[28]

Ultimately Edwards gained the inner strength he needed to kick drugs by falling in love with eighteen-year-old porn girl Renee Summers, who starred in *La Boomba*, *Doctor Ruthless*, *Pony Girls*, *Deep Obsession*, and *Night Heat*. After chasing her for two years, Edwards married Summers in 1986 when she was four months pregnant with his child. They made several good pornos together, including 1988's *In a Crystal Fantasy*. "Renee and Eric consistently combine good sex with good laughter, good acting and good dialog," writes critic Robert Rimmer. "It's a winning combination that makes their sex vids fun to watch."[29]

In 1991, Edwards made his best movie, *Mirage*. "Ashlyn Gere stars as a publishing house liaison to a reclusive author who is overdue with his next book. Edwards weaves one of his couples-oriented stories, and the cast does a wonderful job of fleshing out the plot and still serving up some sizzling hot sex. It's an interesting and well-thought-out feature that will satisfy those who want a little movie with their sex scenes."[30]

Real life romance was much more difficult for Edwards. When Summers gave birth to their first child, the couple resolved to perform in porn no longer. But five days later, Edwards was back in front of the camera.

"One of the saddest aspects of this industry is the marriage situation. Everyone in it seems to want a long-term lasting relationship but the only people they come in contact with are people in the industry," says Edwards. "It's difficult for relationships to last because of the jealousy, especially if you're performing sex with other people."[31] Many of Edwards's peers echo this sentiment.

After several separations from Summers, in 1995 Edwards moved out for good with his two sons. Renee stayed at home with her new boyfriend. Soon after, the house burned down and virtually all of Edwards's belongings were destroyed. "We [Eric and his two boys] had three days' worth of clothes and that was it. We took out the back seat of the van and used it as a sofa. We ate on the floor." "I've been in this business for 27 years," said Edwards in May 1996. "I've paid my dues and I should have people who will hire me and back me up, but I'm constantly having to seek work. Even if it's just being a production assistant and sweeping the floor and cleaning up coffee cups. . . . The trouble is I forgot to pull out. I was so good back in the old days, pulling out and coming all over the belly and face. . . . I just forgot." Edwards laughs, then grows serious. "Somewhere along the line I've lost everything I gathered in life to the women I fell in love with. And here I am hanging pictures on the walls of my tiny apartment with the only love I have left—my boys."[32]

❖❖❖❖

Widely considered America's worst filmmaker, Edward Wood Jr. displayed cinematic discipline and talent leagues beyond most pornographers.

Tim Burton's 1994 bio-pic, *Ed Wood*, tells the true story of the cross-dresser who made *I Changed My Sex* in 1953, and *Plan 9 from Outer Space* in 1959—a film some call the low point of American cinema. Burton, however, does not follow the progress of Wood into pornography. In 1962, Wood wrote *Shotgun Wedding*, a rip-off of the late 1930s flick *Child Bride*. In 1965, Wood helped Stephen C. Apostoloff create *Orgy of the Dead*—the story of evil spirits who return from the grave to perform striptease. In the early 1970s, Wood and Apostoloff made numerous softcore flicks such as *Snow Bunnies*, *Drop-Out Wife*, and *Fugitive Girls*. While Apostoloff refused to go hardcore, Wood, dressed in women's underwear and Angora sweaters, ventured into realms few men had traveled before.

Wood thought porn beneath him and his skin productions include little of the passion he invested in such grandly awful movies as *Plan 9*. His best X-rated film, *Necromania*, appeared in 1971. Shot for $7,000, the 16mm color picture starred Rene Bond, Ric Lutze, and Marie Arnold. Wood made the hardcore scenes in a motel where room temperatures reached 110 degrees. Bond passed out. After receiving a sprinkling of water, she revived enough to suck and fuck Ric Lutze in a coffin.

"*Necromania* exemplifies the trend toward better entertainment in X-rated films," Wood wrote in his book *Censorship, Sex and the Movies*. "When the patron lays down his 3, 5, or whatever bills at the box office he is not going to leave the theater feeling cheated."[33]

Wood pumped out pornographic novels for publishers such as Triumph News, Viceroy Books, and Pendulum to support his thirst for alcohol. Some of his titles include *Devil Girls*, *Death of a Transvestite*, and *Raped in the Grass*. Publisher Bernie Bloom says "Ed's work alone equaled the other four writers [who wrote for Pendulum Publishing]. He had a fantastic imagination. . . . Smoke poured out of the typewriter."[34]

Rudolph Grey, in his book *Nightmare of Ecstasy*, explains how Wood loved to talk women's fashion with Bloom's wife, Blanche. He said if he could have anything in life, he'd come back as a blonde female. Wood was popular with beautiful women, several of whom he married, and although he cross-dressed, he denied ever having gay sex.

Wood produced some of the first Swedish erotica 8mm loops for the pioneering porn producer Caballero. Wood's titles may have included *Massage Parlour*, *Girl Friday*, and *The Jailer*. When *Deep Throat* came out, Wood said, "What the hell was that? I've been writing these for the last six years."[35]

"Ed Wood was a crazy genius," Bloom told Wood biographer Rudolph Grey, author of *Nightmare of Ecstasy*. "Way ahead of his time. Everybody was afraid to do the things he'd do."[36]

Wood wrote and directed a series of twenty-minute hardcore loops on Super 8mm film called *Sex Education Correspondence School*, released in 1975. "They were part of this home study guide Pendulum put out," remembers colleague Charles Anderson. "You'd get these 8mm movies with the books. We did a romantic situation with a husband and wife at home that progressed into hardcore. But it had the pretense of self-help."[37]

Hollywood actor Aldo Ray degenerated into alcoholism in the 1960s and became a regular drinking buddy of Wood. "We talked a lot about life," Ray told Grey. "We agreed to take advantage of the now."[38] Ray became the first Hollywood star to work (clothed) in a pornographic film, appearing in 1977's *Sweet Susan*.

Florence Dolder lived next to Ed Wood in his final years in a dirty little apartment complex on Yucca Street in Hollywood. "The girl upstairs rented out her one child, a girl four or five years of age, to porno movies. Eddie reported it. He was furious. . . . Writing porno was killing him. He was too good for porno. It ate away at him. Eddie was a gentleman."[39] Kathy Wood says her husband loved the song "Amazing Grace," and while deeply depressed he wrote the book *Saving Grace*.

On the morning of December 7, 1978, Los Angeles
County Sheriff deputies evicted Ed and Kathy Wood from
their apartment on Yucca Street. Wood screamed that he had
all kinds of contacts in Hollywood. Then he tried to be nice,
and started pleading for a couple of more hours to call
people. The deputies apologized but said the Woods had to
leave. While Kathy screamed obscenities, Ed slumped down
in the hallway against the wall and cried.

The couple moved in with Ed's actor friend Peter Coe.
Wood downed numerous shots of vodka over the weekend. At
noon on Sunday, December 10, he felt bad and decided to lie
down. When Ed ordered his wife to get him another drink, she
refused. Then he screamed, "Kathy, I can't breathe." Tired of
Ed always telling her what to do, Kathy ignored him. After a
few minutes of quiet, she sent a friend to check on Wood. At
age fifty-four, he was dead of a heart attack.

"I still remember when I went into that room that afternoon and he was dead, his eyes were wide open," says Kathy.
"I'll never forget the look in his eyes. He clutched at the
sheets. It looked like he'd seen hell."[40]

Notes

1. Kenneth Turan and Stephen F. Zito, *Sinema* (New York:
Praeger Publishers, 1974), p. 149.

2. Ibid., p. 152.

3. Ibid., p. 154.

4. Ibid.

5. Ibid., p. 166.

6. Ibid., p. 155.

7. Carol Schatz and Lorenzo Benet, "Sequel: Porn Free for

More Than 20 Years after 'The Devil in Miss Jones,' Georgina Spelvin Is Dried Out and Demonless," *People* (March 13, 1995): 91–92.

8. "Georgina Spelvin," *Adam Film World* (January 1987). The accuracy of all quotes from Spelvin were confirmed by her in a January 1998 letter to the author.

9. Ibid.

10. Ibid.

11. Ibid.

12. Ibid., p. 33.

13. Ibid.

14. Personal interview with Bill Margold, August 1996.

15. *Radical Affairs 6* (Directed by Mark Stone, Moonlight Video, 1993).

16. William Rotsler, *Contemporary Erotic Cinema* (New York: Ballantine Books, 1973), p. 72.

17. Ibid.

18. Turan and Zito, *Sinema*; Robert Rimmer, *The X-Rated Videotape Guide* (Amherst, N.Y.: Prometheus Books, 1993); John Hubner, *Bottom Feeders* (New York: Doubleday, 1992); and personal interview with Marilyn Chambers.

19. Hubner, *Bottom Feeders*, p. 204.

20. Turan and Zito, *Sinema*, p. 162.

21. Ibid.

22. Hubner, *Bottom Feeders*, p. 198.

23. Personal interview with Jim Holliday, April 18, 1996.

24. Quoted in Hubner, *Bottom Feeders*, p. 248.

25. Personal interview with Eric Edwards, May 31, 1996.

26. Ibid.

27. Ibid.

28. Ibid.

29. Robert Rimmer, *X-Rated Videotape Guide II* (Amherst, N.Y.: Prometheus Books, 1991), p. 273.

30. "Mirage," *Adam Film World 1996 Directory*, p. 261.

31. Edwards interview.

32. Ibid.

33. Quoted by Rudolph Grey, *Nightmare of Ecstasy* (Los Angeles: Feral House, 1992), p. 137.

34. Ibid.

35. Ibid.

36. Ibid.

37. Ibid., p. 133.

38. Ibid., p. 144.

39. Ibid., p. 152.

40. Ibid., p. 160.

4.

The Golden Age of Porn

eforc Marilyn Chambers made *Behind the Green Door*, she posed for a new picture for the Ivory soap box. Then in 1973, as revenues for her X-rated movie slumped, Proctor and Gamble released their new box showing Marilyn gazing into the eyes of a baby. Jumping on their own soapbox, the Mitchell brothers sent Chambers to talk shows across America as the 100 percent pure Ivory soap girl.

Though Procter and Gamble finally pulled her picture, replacing it with the idealized drawing of a young woman that remains its cover, Chambers was forever known as the girl on the Ivory soap box, "the perfect symbol of the main-streaming of pornography," notes author John Hubner. "Marilyn was the girl next door who liked sex."[1]

Her performance in *Green Door* became a lightning rod in the debate over pornography. Defenders saw Chambers as a nice girl who discovers herself through sex. Opponents saw her character as enslaved and humiliated, leaving the sex club a robot programmed to say yes. Jim and Artie Mitchell loved the fight because it sold tickets to their film.

At the end of 1974, Marilyn Chambers decided she'd gone as far as she could with the Mitchell brothers and gave her career and life over to her new manager and husband, Chuck Traynor. Chambers was starved for adoration and Traynor convinced her that he knew how to market her talents. Traynor, who had married Chambers in Las Vegas in 1975, initially tried to mainstream her. She starred in Las Vegas plays *Last of the Red Hot Lovers* by Neil Simon and *Mind with a Dirty Man* which ran for a year. Her disco number *Beihana* made the charts in the late 1970s. The only porn star to appear on the cover of *Home Video* magazine, Chambers auditioned for the role of a runaway daughter who becomes a porn star in the mainstream movie *Hardcore*. The casting director told her, "You don't look like a porno queen. You look too clean and wholesome."[2] According to porn historian John Hubner, meeting Hollywood stars at parties and screwing many of them was as close as Marilyn ever really came to mainstream success. Chambers herself confirmed this assessment in an interview in January 1996.

Angry at losing Chambers, the Mitchell brothers patched together outtakes from her previous films and released *Inside Marilyn Chambers* as revenge. Porn historian Robert Rimmer writes,

> While you still won't know what goes on in Marilyn's mind after you have watched this, it's the most interesting of the "Inside" porno star films. Not only Marilyn, but Johnny Keyes and George McDonald discuss the making of *Behind the Green Door* . . . and they give you some insight into their feelings in making porn. Marilyn enjoys acting out her rape fantasies, and Keyes tells how he had five climaxes with Marilyn during one scene, but nevertheless managed to keep thrusting inside her. George McDonald reveals that after having sex with Marilyn for several

hours and not climaxing, he asked her in the shower to relieve him—which she did by hand because her vagina was too sore to continue vaginally.[3]

From 1975 to 1985, Chambers and Traynor criss-crossed the country as Marilyn headlined one porn theater after another. Chuck refused to allow his wife to take classes at the University of Nevada at Las Vegas in case the word got out and it spoiled her image. He limited her intake of alcohol and drugs and forbade her to smoke. "For me to be put on a pedestal," says Chambers, "and adored by millions of men, I loved that. I never felt exploited by Chuck or anybody else. I exploited me."[4]

After *Behind the Green Door* and *Resurrection of Eve*, Marilyn performed in three more adult features—*Insatiable* (1980), *Up 'n Coming* (1983) and *Insatiable 2* (1984). Converted to videotape, these films led the video revolution, staying at the top of the rental charts through 1985.

Tired of Traynor's discipline, Chambers cut loose in 1985, though she was forced by her contract to keep Traynor as her manager and pay him 50 percent of her earnings through 1990. Enjoying her freedom, Chambers resumed smoking, drinking, and using drugs such as cocaine. She went all out in her public performances at the Mitchell Brothers' O'Farrell Theater in San Francisco, enduring heavy whipping and bondage while fellow dancers drove their fists a foot deep into her vagina and ass. Chambers often locked the door in the Kopenhagen lounge (a private room at the O'Farrell) and allowed the patrons to do anything they wanted to her—giving or receiving oral sex, as well as anal and vaginal intercourse.[5]

Paving her way to an early grave, consuming massive amounts of alcohol and cocaine, Chambers met her husband-to-be, Tom Taylor, on a blind date in 1986. "It was lust at first sight," remembers Chambers, who felt stunned when

Taylor didn't realize who she was.[6] They had a great first date, but then Taylor called to say he couldn't see her again. A recovering heroin addict, he'd taken a vow not to associate with anyone who used drugs. Chambers got so angry that she kicked a wall and broke her leg. Taylor visited her in the hospital and Chambers ended up in Narcotics Anonymous. She says she's been clean and sober since 1988.

"It was difficult for me to meet men who didn't have this preconceived notion about me, or else were totally intimidated and shaking. Tom had no idea who I was. He'd never heard of me. I was crushed. I thought I was famous. But he cracked me up. He made me laugh so hard I was rolling on the floor. At first he was appalled when his friends asked him, 'Do you know who Marilyn Chambers is?' and showed him. Now it's a turn-on for him."[7]

Chambers told the *Chicago Tribune* in June 1989 that AIDS drew the curtain on her porn career. "I was offered a lot of money to do another X-rated film, a lot more than my normal asking price, which was $100,000. But I'm not willing to die for it.

"There's tons of new, young girls in the business now, and you just wonder, don't they listen to TV or read the newspapers? A lot of them think it's a fast buck, but you're playing with your life now."[8]

In 1990, Chambers gave birth to a girl whom she wants to keep out of porn; Chambers regrets her X-rated past. "It's gotten me to where I am today, but if I were to do things over again, I'd do them differently."[9]

❖❖❖❖

"Pink films," as pornos are known in Japan, began to be made early in the twentieth century. The year 1972, however, ushered in movies about real sex, just as *Deep Throat* played a similar role in America. From the 1950s through the 1990s, American magazines bore the brunt of the legal assault against sexual entertainment. In Japan, by contrast, major movie studios led the struggle against censorship. In 1972, that country's oldest studio reinvented itself as a soft-porn producer. At the time the country's slumping box office forced five major production companies out of business. On the verge of bankruptcy, Nikkatsu Corporation made *roman poruno*—romantic softcore films. Nikkatsu used respectable budgets, innovative camera angles, superb acting, and strong plots to produce films which won acclaim for their quality despite facing unusual legal restrictions. Based on notions written into law by American occupiers after World War II, Japan's Motion Picture Code of Ethics Committee prohibited exposure of the genitals. In response, Japanese directors followed their peers around the world by airbrushing out explicit sex while pouring on the violence.

Japan's best known porno, and perhaps the best sexually explicit film ever—*In the Realm of the Senses*—is one film whose hardcore scenes had to be airbrushed in order for the picture to be released there. A sensation of the mid-1970s, *Realm* dramatized the true story of a World War II–era prostitute who walked around the streets of Tokyo for several days with a man's cut-off penis in her hand. *Magill's Survey of Cinema* calls the 1976 flick a "fascinating study of radical extremes. . . . Sada (Eiko Matsuda) and Kichi (Tatsuya Fuji) engage in incessant and shameless copulation which excites servant girls, geishas, and others around them bound to the workaday world. Kichi becomes increasingly anxious to please Sada, and, to prolong his erections, she repeatedly strangles him, until, as they both seem to foresee, he dies."[10]

The director, Nagisa Oshima, led the Japanese New Wave

which began in the early 1960s. A prolific writer of mani-
festoes, Oshima, born in 1932, despised the traditional work
of Akira Kurosawa, Yasufjiro Ozu, and the other postwar hu-
manists. A student radical, he eventually substituted nihilism
for communism. "I am not a Marxist. I find Marxism and
Christianity to be the same thing, and both of them are bad.[11]

"I no longer know who I am," said Oshima. "That's the
subject of my films." The surrealist filmmaker loved to explore criminal and deviant behavior but after *Realm* he
turned his back on porn. In 1983 he released the mainstream
Merry Christmas Mr. Lawrence, and in 1985 *Max Mon
Amour*. Neither attracted much attention.

During the 1980s, porn in Japan, as in the rest of the
world, relapsed into formula.

In Europe, shortly after the release of *Behind the Green
Door*, Lasse Braun shot his first feature, the quasi-documen-
tary *French Blue*, showcasing his protegée Brigitte Maier. In
1974, *Blue* became the first hardcore to appear at the Cannes
Film Festival. During the first two months of 1975, Braun
made his masterpiece *Sensations* with $250,000 from his
American friend Reuben Sturman. Bill Margold and Jim
Holliday rank this Brigitte Maier vehicle as the best non-
American porn film ever.

"Lasse Braun is . . . an eccentric genius who shoots mas-
terful sex films when he's in top form," says Holliday. "*Sensations* demonstrates that there is nothing better than a great
foreign film. I would rate this French film as the hottest foreign entry ever made, and even on a professional level, *Sensations* belongs in the all-time top five . . . so sumptuous that
sex is an art."[12]

A beautiful French woman, Sylvia Bourdon, one of
Braun's lovers, recruited so many of her compatriots
(Veronique Monet, Frederick Barral, Pierre Latour, Nicole

Velna, and Jean Villroy, then in his sixties) for *Sensations* that many thought the project a French film. It wasn't, though metaphorically "French films" are synonymous with "blue films," which are synonymous with porn.

Once France overthrew Gaullist censorship in the early 1970s, porn features such as *Exhibition*, *Kinky Ladies of Bourbon Street*, *The Felines*, *Pussy Talk*, and *Candy's Candy* poured forth, and in 1975, sex films accounted for a quarter of all French movie production.[13] Worried about its country's image, the French Ministry of Culture in 1977 banned export of porn films.

❖❖❖❖

In one sense, the American pornographer has a friend in the United States government. With varying effectiveness, American customs agents through the 1990s routinely seized hardcore imports such as Oshima's *In the Realm of the Senses*, which was on its way to the New York Film Festival in 1976. But unlike France and England, the United States does not restrict porn shipped abroad.

Softcore artist Radley Metzger, who directed *Therese and Isabelle*, *Carmen Baby*, *Score*, *The Lickerish Quartet*, and other films, used the porn name Henry Paris when he made his first explicit film, 1974's *The Private Afternoons of Pamela Mann*, which moved porn films to near–Hollywood quality. "*The Private Afternoons of Pamela Mann*," wrote Bill Margold in 1975, "signals an end to the all-balling, no purpose, disposable mastur-movies that go into one orifice and out another."[14]

Released in 1975, Metzger's *The Opening of Misty Beethoven* received the first annual Erotic Film Festival Award for Best Movie, and it is generally regarded by critics as the best porn movie ever. Loosely based on George Bernard

Shaw's *Pygmalion*, *Misty* stars Jamie Gillis and Constance Money,* who performed in only eight X-rated movies.

Money says she expected *The Opening of Misty Beethoven* to be an R-rated picture. "*Misty* is a good movie because it is real," Money told *Adam* magazine. She claimed the incidents in the film happened to her at the time, especially her relationship with Jamie Gillis. "Henry Paris made me that character. He told me I couldn't 'act.' "[15]

Money claims she neither got paid for *Misty Beethoven* nor did she sign a release.

> I didn't have a good attitude and I didn't like Henry Paris. Henry makes films with blood. Not money, blood. The man is sick. Anyone who squirts somebody in the face with K-Y Jelly and cottage cheese for ten hours a day has got to be doing it for more than just film.
>
> Jamie [Gillis] beat me up sexually. Jamie and I had and still have a strange relationship. He's kinky. My sexual learning is just as *Misty Beethoven* showed. I started off clumsy. . . .
>
> Having done these films affects my relationships which is why I retired. A guy I'm going out with might go to a stag party where they show a tape, and other guys will say, "Isn't that your girlfriend?" It's hard for them to deal with it because most of them are really straight.[16]

Although Money retired to the Pacific Northwest for several years, in 1982 she made *A Taste of Money*, a romantic account of her return to X. Money then reverted to her real name and moved to Alaska to run a restaurant.

Misty Beethoven and other pornographic features accounted for about 16 percent of the total American movie box office between the years of 1972 and 1983.[17] Counting revenues from peep shows, pornos grossed about half the

---

*Metzger says he bestowed the porn name "Constance Money" on his *Misty Beethoven* star because she constantly asked him for money.

amount of their Hollywood counterparts. Figuring out who got what, however, verges on the impossible due to results of the Supreme Court's 1973 *Miller* ruling. "The open nature of pornography distribution in the broad sweeps of legal market territory throughout Europe, combined with the general willingness of leading figures there to discuss financial detail, makes it a relatively straightforward task to map out the contours of supply and demand, price and profit," write the authors of the 1988 book *Porn Gold*. "In the United States, where interpretative definitions of 'obscenity' and 'pornography' have created a legal minefield, the opposite is true."[18]

With over one hundred new porn features in 1976, *Time* magazine issued a cover story on April 5 of that year entitled "The Porno Plague," complaining that every major American city now featured "a garish, grubby, mile-long gauntlet of sex-book stalls, theaters and 8-mm peep shows for voyeurs, and massage parlors and sexual encounter centers for those who want direct action."[19] Still, according to Phil Paresi, one of the original distributors of *Deep Throat*, demand fell so drastically by 1976, compared to just two years before, that the average production earned no more than $300,000 in rentals, not a great return if expenses are high and profits must be divided among several investors.

To keep up sales, producers took out full-page ads in *Variety* touting "new" techniques like 3-D, and sending popular performers like Marilyn Chambers, Leslie Bovee, Linda Wong, and C.J. Laing on promotional tours with their movies. But it wasn't enough.

This financial slump came just as X-rated movies became more professional—a confusing fact to those who don't realize the lack of connection between artistry and profit. In porn, artistry matters only to the degree it induces an erection.

In addition to declining demand, pornographers faced two main challenges—the uncertainty of national distribution and the proliferation of softcore. Threatened by federal legal intervention and local zoning ordinances, distribution networks were dominated by the Mafia. Those filmmakers such as the Mitchell brothers, who at times avoided working with the Mob, suffered heavy losses when their prints were pirated.

As one of *Variety*'s top-grossing films of 1976, *Alice in Wonderland* exemplified the second challenge to the hardcore industry, the proliferation of quasirespectable softcore. For example, veteran American producer-director Jonas Middleton made 1973's *Illusions of a Lady*. Then he raised $200,000 and assembled a cast of fifty for the arty *Through the Looking Glass* which was publicized in *Playboy* and *Penthouse*. Ads read: "A film that is aimed at the same sophisticated couples market that was attracted to last year's *Emmanuelle*."

Middleton shot *Through the Looking Glass* in one hard and two soft versions so that it could be distributed to three different types of audiences. He sold rights to his film to exhibitors in Europe and Asia, and Dell published a novel based on the script. Middleton stressed the literary origins— a Russian short story—of his film. "I'm trying to upgrade the genre," he said, "and get into a sophisticated plot." He preferred to call the results a "psychological thriller, supernatural sex, not really a porno."[20] That many pornographers such as Middleton don't want to call porn porn reflects the genre's abysmal reputation. In fact, Compton's encyclopedia begins its entry on pornography with the phrase "Perhaps the lowest level of artistic or literary endeavor."

Bob Rimmer called *Through the Looking Glass* "a terrific gothic drama. . . . Middleton gives you a fifteen-minute cinematographic tour of madness that might have been inspired by

Hieronymus Bosch's paintings. It will scare the hell out of you—or make you want to throw up."[21] *Looking Glass* matched the nihilistic zeitgeist of the 1970s. Despite the attempts to improve porn's reputation—by basing storylines in classic literature, or by employing high-class models in starring roles, for example—the genre is still a refuge of narcissism.

"Whatever the talents lavished on porn," wrote academic Joseph Slade in the late 1970s, "so far their shades of blue do not add up to a coherent spectrum. Craft and crudity war: If a director achieves silky, poetic cinema tones or choreographs bodies balletically, he will blow the continuity or fail in something else. Below the top level, all porn features are dogs, and there is little point in picking best of breed. Even the slickest share faults, scenes held too long, excessive close-ups of genitals, jerky editing, under-lighting, out-of-sync sound tracks."[22]

While mainstream films shoot as much as twenty feet of film for every one foot used, X-rated features depend on a two-to-one ratio. Like any formula genre, porn forever turns back upon itself to imitate the tradition from which it derives. Dozens of pornos appear each year about the making of pornos, allowing for quick nudity and sex. Such a scheme adds the excitement of voyeurism as the "real" camera follows photographers filming the action. In *China Girl*, Asian villains video-monitor the sex of prominent scientists while in *The Double Exposure of Holly*—note the title—videotapes of her affairs ruin a haughty wife.

One formidable obstacle to porn as quality cinema is the fleeting nature of eroticism, which is why directors like Gregory Dark compose their movies in self-contained, ten-minute segments. After you've gotten off, there's little reason to continue watching a porno. Successive orgasmic climaxes weaken dramatic ones. Thus, a formula suited for a stag film may not work in a feature, which must delay gratification.

✦✦✦✦

The year 1978 produced more good X-rated movies than any other, including *Anna Obsessed*, *Candy Stripers*, *Debbie Does Dallas*, *The Health Spa*, *Skin Flicks*, *China Cat*, *The Joy of Fooling Around*, and *Slave to Pleasure*. Porn features accounted for 17 percent of the $365 million box office.[23] *Debbie Does Dallas* became one of the five best selling pornos of all time, providing relief from the diet of depressing X-rated material that marked the Golden Age.

Powerful stars like Annette Haven and Vanessa Del Rio, along with directors like Anthony Spinelli and Alex deRenzy, set a standard for porn excellence during the late 1970s that Jim Holliday and others believe has never been equalled. "If anti-pornography forces even begin to comprehend that this entire industry is run by 'the power of the pussy,' " writes Holliday, "they would leave it alone."[24]

Porn's Golden Age features distinguished themselves in the following ways:

- Golden Age films shot on film, a superior medium to video because of its higher quality and sharper pictures that convey more depth and feeling.
- Played on a big screen, Golden Age films provided complete cinematic experiences with plot, location, dialogue, and production values. Though pornographers shot numerous loops and compilations during the 1970s as well, the best twenty films of each year compared to their video followers demonstrate more of a "movie" feel.
- Film uses fewer close-ups than productions designed for TV screens. That's why Golden Age films that have

been transferred to video produce sex scenes that feel like they're shot from thirty feet away.

- Golden Age films boasted budgets of hundreds of thousands of dollars, several times the amount spent on any pornographic production since 1984. Typical budgets of 1976 films—$200,000 each—would translate to over a million dollars each in today's money. The highest budgeted 1,000 films of the 1970s spent about twenty times as much as their 1990s counterparts.

- Golden Age films are long on story because they were made for exhibition in theaters, where viewers can rarely masturbate and never fast-forward.

- Golden Age performers appeared more natural. "These are not the bronzed, implanted, shaved, perfectly buffed bodies of the nineties," writes critic Steve Brent. "These women look like real people . . . like the amateurs of today."[25]

- Los Angeles produced less than 40 percent of the Golden Age films while the area now makes 90 percent of America's porno. This alone accounts for many of the differences between porn before 1985 and after. Los Angeles concentrates on light productions of fun sex while New York produced darker, more thoughtful films like the original *Devil in Miss Jones*. San Francisco experimented with "artistic porn."

- In the quasi-legal environment of the 1970s and early 1980s, pornographers experimented with explicit depictions of violence, rape, bestiality, fisting, urination, and children.

- Porn directors and crews of the 1970s frequently came from mainstream film backgrounds.

- Golden Age pornographers usually scripted their sex.

Instead of using the documentarian approach of video and winging it, Golden Age filmmakers moved cameras and lighting and edited their movies in the bay (an editing facility) instead of on the set. "They blocked out their scenes more carefully because film is more expensive and more difficult to shoot," notes journalist Hart Williams. "Video feels more slapdash."[26]

• Golden Age pornographers harbored more illusions about their medium, frequently believing that films of explicit sex promoted a loving world. Golden Age films made more "statements" than today's videos.

• Of all technical qualities, sound has long suffered the most in porn. Few Golden Age films played the audio portions of their sex scenes. Most overlayed them with classical music.

Hart Williams concludes,

The Golden Age tried to make "films," the video age tries to make a buck. There was enough money in porn [in the 1970s] that artistic concerns could take a front seat. As long as "the Pussycat would play it," you could pretty much do anything. Video, by contrast, was almost entirely "entrepreneur" driven: not much money to make a lot of cash. I remember when Bill Margold . . . shot *Fantasy Follies* for $30,000. Nobody liked it [it was savaged by most reviewers], but producers thought, "It's only thirty grand? I gotta do a video!" By 1986, they had fundamentally taken a zero off of production costs (though many kept mindlessly trying to do "film" production using video, which is like trying to do oil technique with charcoal pencils —pointless and idiotic): $100K to $10K. Video was not lucrative for long, so from the beginning, there was a cheapskate mentality.[27]

"One of the great delusions of the 1970s," wrote Maitland McDonaugh in 1996, "was that movie audiences wanted to see upscale hardcore movies with plots and production values; the home-video revolution of the '80s dispelled that notion. People who really want to see sex fast-forward past anything that smacks of narrative."[28]

Paul Thomas Anderson's 1997 Hollywood picture, *Boogie Nights*, dramatizes porn's shift from film to video. The godfather character appears to be an amalgam of the late Carlo Gambino, leader of the Gambino family, and Reuben Sturman, each of whom foresaw the huge profit potential of the video revolution. *Boogie Nights* character director Jack Anderson, played by Burt Reynolds, resembles such pornographers as Henri Pachard, Bob Chinn, Anthony Spinelli, and Lasse Braun, all of whom who had to be dragged into the video age by their money men.

The sharp contrast between two leading sex performers of the Golden Age, Vanessa Del Rio and Annette Haven, parallels the contrast between film and video, metaphorically speaking. Haven, an ice princess, rarely lost control while Del Rio went balls out, portraying sluts.

Born in 1952, Puerto Rican Anna Maria Sanchez began her porn career in the early 1970s. The future Vanessa Del Rio first appeared on the big screen in 1974's *Cherry Hustlers* while her first big role came in *Midnight Desires*, where she sucks down two cocks at once. The lusty Latina would do anything. For a magazine shoot, Vanessa sucked milk out of a cow's udders. She also starred in several loops with Luis Short-Studd, a dwarf, including one in which he slipped his fist up her ass.

Sanchez attended Roman Catholic day schools where she washed, starched, and ironed the nuns' and priests' vestments. Preferring fun to study, she busted loose in high school, losing her virginity in her freshman year. "My boyfriend was eighteen and a virgin like me," Del Rio told the magazine *Adam*.

We went to this porno movie house. The manager didn't care how old we were as long as we paid our two bucks. The theater showed triple features, but back then the type of fucking they did was with their underwear on, and usually they were under the covers. . . . But it was hot for the times.

We sat in the balcony and my boyfriend pulled his cock out of his pants and wrapped my hand around it and taught me to jerk him off. We did this a few times, and finally we went back to his place when his parents weren't home and fucked our brains out. From that time on, it was fuck, fuck, fuck whenever and wherever I could.[29]

A free spirit, Del Rio spent two years traveling around with a guy in his VW bus.

We were outlaws. I worked as a barmaid and a go-go dancer, and that opened me up. Then a friend of mine called me up and asked me if I wanted to go to Sweden on short notice. He said I'd make fuck films at fifty dollars per film and three films a day.

I was so excited and I needed money. I didn't know anything about acting but I sure knew how to fuck. Before I knew it, I was in the movies and I went nuts. I fucked everyone on the set, including the cameraman.[30]

In other interviews, Del Rio doesn't sound nearly as enthusiastic about her time in porn, saying that she only did it because her family needed the money. Generally speaking, porn queens, like the rest of us, say what people want to hear.

Porn's first gorgeous woman, Annette Haven, born in 1953, featured a body in the soft 1970s mold rather than the sculpted 1990s look. "None of today's porn girls are classy like Annette," says William Rotsler. "She's a rarity in this genre."[31] In her lack of enthusiasm for sex, however, the Jane Seymore lookalike typifies the performances of porn's most attractive. "It's the Annette Haven school of acting," explains Holliday. "I'm a 10 and I know I'm a 10, and so I'm just going to lie here and allow myself to get penetrated."[32]

Haven grew up a Mormon but soon rebelled against her religiously and politically conservative upbringing. "A classic beauty and a mind as sharp as a stiletto set her apart," writes *AFW*. "Haven's roles ranged from innocent virgin to bitchy executive, and her commitment to excellence is apparent in her unwavering concentration on the task at hand, whether it be delineating a character or pumping a dick."[33]

In later years, Haven played professional women unafraid of their sexuality. Her best movie may be *Tower of Power*, in which she portrays a high-level executive struggling for control of a major corporation. Even as Herschel Savage pumps her ferociously, she maintains control. "The script called for him to submit," remembers Annette, "but he wouldn't. He wouldn't budge, so I threw him to the floor, which wasn't in the script. It surprised the hell out of him."[34]

Public Affairs presents Haven as an investigative reporter who exposes a corrupt candidate. "The first time I worked with Richard Pacheco, I was so overwhelmed by my orgasm that I fainted. When I came to, Richard was holding me in his arms. Everyone else had gone home."[35]

"She is a strong woman," writes *AFW*, "and that may be daunting to some men, but her fans love that she can be so outspoken, yet dynamically sexual. She's a thinking man's sex goddess: always sexy, ever a lady."[36]

Unusual among porn girls, Haven refused to swallow during cum shots. Long retired, she retains her ice princess demeanor. The veteran of more than seventy-five movies claims, "I never called anyone for a role; they all called me." She says she'd still be doing videos today if everyone practiced safe sex. "I'm a strict person and you have to work within my parameters."[37]

Jesie St. James also set strict limits on pornographers. "I don't do anal sex," she told *Adam*. "I've never had it privately and it's not something that I'd be willing to do for the camera. And S&M . . . I'll beat the shit out of anybody else, but they won't lay a hand on me."[38]

St. James, who turned in one of porn's all-time performances in the Anthony Spinelli film *Easy*, felt annoyed that most see the penis as being the main ingredient of a sex scene.

> I would like to do away with those close-ups. You should be able to see enough of the insertion without having to focus in on that area. It's not erotic to me. It's clinical. I might as well be at a doctor's office seeing slides. There's no excitement. That's why I don't do loops.
>
> I'd like to see more sensuality and eroticism. More foreplay—which can be erotic, building up to a climax. I don't like the whole formula for adult films. They start with a little story at the beginning, then they have one sex scene, then they'll go to another little story and get another sex scene and then they'll flash back—this one will be having an orgasm—then the next one, etc. . . . They should start with their whole story and save a lot of the orgasms for the end of the movie.
>
> People come to see X films to be teased. They come to be stimulated instead of just—boom—throwing it all out there in the beginning. If they would get into the story and tease people along for the first three-quarters of the film, saving the explicit action for the end, they would have a turn-on.[39]

Like St. James, most porn girls want more scripts, character development, and romance. They want fewer cum shots and graphic close-ups. In essence, they don't want porn.

> If I go to see a sex film, I want it to appeal to what I like. And what I like is to be in control. If a man goes to an X-rated film, he wants to see the man in control. He's got this gorgeous woman who's deprived of sex and will do anything to have sex with him and he doesn't have to do a thing. So it's appealing to a male audience. But I think they should open up the whole industry and give women like [director] Gail Palmer the opportunity to present the woman's point of view.[40]

❖❖❖❖

In 1972, Hollywood's most powerful talent agency, William Morris, signed rich kid Phil Tobias. After his appearances on Broadway in *Jesus Christ Superstar* and other productions, Tobias appeared ready for TV and movie work, but instead he entered porn and took the name Paul Thomas.

He enjoyed his new status as a big fish in a small pond. While Phil Tobias was another struggling actor, "Paul Thomas" was a star, albeit a porn star. At times, however, he and his family felt disappointment with his choosing the easy way out. What a loss of potential. What might have been?

> There's the stigma that comes with my profession. Being everything from a gigolo to a prostitute to a no-good immoral son of a bitch means that at any time, if someone is angry at you for something totally unrelated to films, they'll grab that hook "X-rated films." It's an easy one to grab.
>
> On the other hand, if somebody wants to look at the films in a beneficial vein, there's a lot of wonderful things to say about them. But again, it is something that someone can jump on if they want to get on my case. And depending who it is coming from, depending on my mood, it can get to me. I'll eventually get it together and defend my work and defend the place of erotic films.
>
> I want to defend the films because I want to be respected and I want people to be proud of me. One of the biggest disadvantages of working in erotic films is that you constantly have to explain yourself. It's caused me problems with women. The last women I've been with are not in the business and, given their druthers, would rather that I weren't either. But I'm not about to stop for them.[41]

While starring in the San Francisco play *Beach Blanket Babylon*, Thomas appeared in his first porn feature—1976's *Autobiography of a Flea*. Working in X had long been a fantasy. "Long before I starred in them, I'd go see them in Chicago and

New York. I knew it was something I wanted to do. . . . When I've finished a sex scene, someone will come up to me and say, 'Good job, Paul, good job.' But what did I do? I fucked some beautiful woman. It's the easiest thing in the world. When I act and do a scene well, then I accept and expect congratulations."[42] Although a decent actor, while limp Thomas created few scenes of sexual heat. During the 1990s, however, he shot more pornos on film (as opposed to video) than any American and made more money than any of his peers.

❖❖❖❖

Los Angeles's Weston family, generally known by their stage name of Spinelli, is the first family of porn; the genre's most successful and influential family. They crafted many of the best porn films, including *Night Caller, Sex World, Easy, Talk Dirty to Me, Nothing to Hide*, and the 1982 film often cited as the industry's high water mark, *The Dancers*. Porn director "Anthony Spinelli" grew up as Sam Weinstein. Along with his brother Jack, a well known character actor in Hollywood who died in 1995, Sam changed his last name to Weston to avoid sounding too Jewish.[43]

According to porn star Kay Parker and other sources, Sam Weston created the superb 1964 mainstream film *One Potato, Two Potato*. The movie credits a "Larry Pierce" as its director and Sam as an actor. *Potato*'s controversial theme about interracial love denied it American distribution and supposedly limited Weston's mainstream acting career. To make money, he began shooting porn on 16mm film in 1970. Over the next twenty-four years, largely under the moniker "Anthony Spinelli," Weston made most of L.A.'s best hardcore films, receiving help from the late 1970s onward from his sons Mitch and Michael.

"Good directors are like good fathers," writes *AFW*,

"they find the right balance between giving their children (cast and crew) guidance, and giving them room to find their own way. The best father is reassuring, warm, humorous, firm without being too authoritarian. [Anthony] Spinelli is all these things. . . . Character interests Spinelli so much, that all of his movies are about people, not merely types."[44]

Renee Bond and Ric Lutze star in Spinelli's first 35mm feature, *Touch Me* (1971), about an encounter group weekend. Few theaters dared show Spinelli's 1972 film *An Act of Confession*, the story of a nun preparing for her final vows while still troubled by erotic dreams. The confession with the priest turns into group sex while the taking of communion becomes a blow job for the altar boy and the priest. Another scene shows the heroine tied to a cross while she's ravaged by two friars. Later Christ appears walking on water while receiving a blow job. Some critics rank *Confession*, along with Spinelli's *Night Caller* (1975) and *Sex World* (1978) among the ten most underrated pornos of all time.

In 1984, Spinelli prefigured the amateur revolution (perhaps best exemplified by shows such as *America's Funniest Home Videos*) with *Reel People*. The veteran director introduces the film and uses porn performers Juliet Anderson, Gail Sterling, Priscilla Shields, John Leslie, Richard Pacheco, and Paul Thomas as foils to allow real people to talk about their sexual selves, their fantasies—and to realize them on camera.

The shift to video, with its hasty shooting schedules and low budgets, was awkward at first for careful directors like Spinelli, but slowly he acquired the light, improvisatory touch needed for one-day wonders. He never followed up on video, however, with his *Reel People* amateur breakthrough, and eventually the business passed him and his sons by. Alzheimer's disease forced Spinelli's retirement in 1994 and three years later his son Mitchell sold the family's production company.

❖❖❖❖

The success of Golden Age hardcore gradually rendered passé softcore entertainment by such institutions as *Playboy* and directors such as Russ Meyer. The circulation of skin magazines peaked in the mid-1970s. *Playboy* fell from 7 million buyers in the last half of 1972 to 5 million in 1977. *Viva*'s and *Playgirl*'s circulation steadily dropped from 1974 and *Viva* soon went out of business. In the last half of 1977, all the major sex magazines except *Penthouse* and *Gallery* suffered declining sales. Those two magazines' big fall lay ahead.[45]

With a monthly circulation of 16 million, the ten leading sex magazines generated close to half a billion dollars in revenue in 1978, over 80 percent from circulation alone. The 780 adult film theaters grossed a similar amount of money, according to *Parade* magazine (August 19, 1979). Sex toys racked up about $100 million in sales while peep shows around the country brought in about $2 billion.[46] By 1979, Hugh Hefner had accumulated a net worth of $150 million. Other millionaires from the sex industry included Bob Guccione, David Friedman, and Russ Meyer.

Known as the King of Nudies and the Barnum of Boobs, Meyer could have retired young and in comfort. But Meyer —the Hugh Hefner of adult films—kept working because of the "hard-on" he got when shooting a good scene with one of his big-breasted female stars: "I'm obsessed with female breasts. . . . They do a lot for me. They titillate me, turn me on, excite me, rejuvenate me." But Meyer was not the type of guy who reduced women to their tits. "I've had more than my share of ass," says Meyer. "And they were all great looking broads."[47]

Meyer believes that his best film is 1970's *Beyond the Valley of the Dolls*, written by frustrated moviemaker-turned-film critic

Roger Ebert. Critics, however, disagree. The story describes the rise of a female rock group against the sleazy background of Hollywood, and is an "atrocious film with all the faults of a Russ Meyer picture and little of his usual virtues," says Rotsler, summing up critical reaction to the movie.[48]

Meyer's last feature film was 1979's *Beyond the Valley of the Ultravixens*. Since then he's embarked on several ambitious projects but finished none. His work in softcore and exploitation has been overshadowed: "As soon as the porno people came in," Meyer said in 1996, "I couldn't find a place to play."[49]

Despite burgeoning competition in the late 1970s, San Francisco's Mitchell brothers kept playing. Low on cash after the commercial and artistic failure of *Sodom and Gomorrah*, Jim Mitchell developed a series called *Ultrakore*—a return to the loops that dominated pornography when the Mitchell brothers broke in. Porn was no longer chic, fewer couples came to the O'Farrell, and the raincoaters grew bored with features built around stupid plots.

Shot on 35mm film, *Ultrakore* made fun of porn. For example, "Hot Nazis" burlesques sadomasochism, portraying female Nazis with fake German accents chanting "We are hot Nazis, we are hot Nazis." When *Ultrakore* burned itself out, the brothers returned to features. *CB Mamas* capitalized on the citizen's band (CB) radio craze. *The Grafenberg Spot* was "a six-day wonder made to raise money for legal expenses" according to Artie. In the sequel, *The Grafenberg Girls Go Fishing*, dildos protrude from anuses and vaginas "like terrible spikes" writes Hubner, "and the sound track has more lowing than a dairy farm at feeding time."[50]

The Mitchells' inability to develop as filmmakers cost them key employees. One quit after saying "fucking cocksucker" to a grandmother he loved and realizing how coarse he'd become. Others tired of grinding out sex films. George McDonald retired because he got sick of acting in them.[51]

The Mitchells showed just as good a business sense leaving the genre as they had when entering. By the early 1980s VCRs began to sell widely and porn fans no longer needed to go to theaters to watch sex. The mainstreaming of pornography that Jim and Artie helped create was complete.[52]

Notes

1. John Hubner, *Bottom Feeders* (New York: Doubleday, 1992), p. 201.

2. Ibid., p. 306. The accuracy of Hubner's quotes and descriptions of Chambers were confirmed by Chambers on January 7, 1996.

3. Robert Rimmer, *The X-Rated Videotape Guide* (Amherst, N.Y.: Prometheus Books, 1993), p. 222.

4. Hubner, *Bottom Feeders*, p. 305.

5. Ibid., pp. 305–309.

6. Clarence Peterson, "Porn? Rate It 'Ex' for Marilyn Chambers," *Chicago Tribune*, June 2, 1989.

7. Ibid.

8. Ibid.

9. Hubner, *Bottom Feeders*, p. 399.

10. "In the Realm of the Senses," *Magill's Survey of Cinema*, June 15, 1995.

11. Ibid.

12. Quoted by David Hebditch and Nick Anning, *Porn Gold* (London: Faber & Faber, 1988), p. 208.

13. "France Discovers Porn," *Oui* (April 1976): 82–91.

14. Bill Margold, "The Private Afternoons of Pamela Mann," *Hollywood Press* (April 1975): 21.

15. "Constance Money," *Adam* (May 1980): 17.

16. Ibid.

17. John Heidenry, *What Wild Ecstasy* (New York: Simon & Schuster, 1997), p. 210.

18. Hebditch and Anning, *Porn Gold*, pp. 70–71.

19. "The Porno Plague," *Time* (April 5, 1976).

20. Jonas Middleton interviewed by Alex Bennet on "Midnight Blue's America," Channel J, Teleprompter TV, New York City, October 2, 1976.

21. Rimmer, *The X-Rated Videotape Guide*, pp. 212–13.

22. Joseph Slade, "The Porn Market and Porn Formulas: The Feature Film of the Seventies," *Journal of Popular Film* 6, issue 2 (1977): 173.

23. Heidenry, *What Wild Ecstasy*, p. 210.

24. Jim Holliday, *Only the Best* (Van Nuys, Calif.: Cal Vista Direct, Ltd., 1986), p. 112.

25. Steve and Elizabeth Brent, *Couples Guide to the Best Erotic Videos* (New York: St. Martin's Press, 1997), p. 99.

26. Personal e-mail to the author from Hart Williams, June 1997.

27. Ibid.

28. Maitland McDonagh, *The 50 Most Erotic Films of All Time* (New York: Citadel Press, 1996), p. 8.

29. "Vanessa Del Rio," *Adam* (May 1980): 38.

30. Ibid.

31. Personal interview with William Rotsler, May 15, 1996.

32. Personal interview with Jim Holliday, April 18, 1996.

33. "Annette Haven," *Adam Film World* (March 1987): 59.

34. Ibid.

35. Ibid.

36. Ibid.

37. "Jamie Gillis Teaches 'Porn Shooting for Beginners' Course, *Adult Video News* (September 1994): 54.

38. "Jesie St. James," *Adam* (June 1980).

39. Ibid.

40. Ibid.

41. "Paul Thomas," *Adam Film World* (August 1983): 23–24.

42. Ibid.

43. "The Spinelli Family," http://www.lukeford.com/c23.html (August 1997).

44. "Anthony Spinelli," *Adam Film World* (July 1987): 36.

45. Heidenry, *What Wild Ecstasy*, p. 204.

46. Michael Satchell, "The Big Business of Selling Smut," *Parade*, August 19, 1979.

47. Rimmer, *The X-Rated Videotape Guide*, p. 152.

48. William Rotsler, *Contemporary Erotic Cinema* (New York: Ballantine Books, 1973), p. 35.

49. Dana Kennedy, "Up Front and Personal: Cult Director Russ Meyer," *Entertainment Weekly* (April 5, 1996): 90.

50. Hubner, *Bottom Feeders*, p. 249.

51. Hubner, *Bottom Feeders*, p. 203.

52. Ibid.

5.

La Cosa Nostra

*O*rganized crime has long played a significant role in porn distribution. Numerous American law enforcement agencies during the 1970s and 1980s, including the Department of Justice and the Task Force on Organized Crime created by the Law Enforcement Assistance Administration, as well as President Reagan's Meese Commission, declared that the Mafia controlled porn.[1] "You cannot be in the field and distribute pornography without their consent," said FBI agent Homer Young in 1986.[2] Similar testimony is provided by the 1986 Attorney General's Commission on Pornography (best known as the Meese Commission after President Ronald Reagan's attorney general of the time Edwin Meese).

Retired FBI agent William P. Kelly told the Meese Commission, "In my opinion, based upon twenty-three years of experience in pornography and obscenity investigations and study, it is practically impossible to be in the retail end of the pornography industry without dealing in some fashion with organized crime."[3]

Officer Thomas Bohling of the Chicago Police Department Organized Crime Division reported, "It is the belief of state, federal, and local law enforcement that the pornography industry is controlled by organized crime families. If they do not own the business outright, they most certainly extract street tax from independent smut peddlers."[4]

Los Angeles Police Chief Daryl F. Gates told the Meese Commission, "Organized crime infiltrated the pornography industry in Los Angeles in 1969 due to its lucrative financial benefits. By 1975, organized crime controlled 80 percent of the industry and it is estimated that this figure is between 85 and 90 percent today.[5]

Based upon such evidence, the 1986 Meese Commission echoed the findings of such earlier reports as the 1978 FBI Report Regarding the Extent of Organized Crime Involvement in Pornography, concluding that

> organized crime involvement in pornography . . . is indeed significant, and there is an obvious national control directly and indirectly by organized crime figures of that industry in the United States. Few pornographers can operate in the United States independently without some involvement with organized crime. The huge profits gathered by organized crime in this area and redirected to other lucrative forms of crime, such as narcotics and investment in legitimate business enterprises, are certainly cause for national concern.[6]

Through the early 1990s, many organized crime experts considered the American Mafia, which is also known as La Cosa Nostra (which means "our thing"), the most dangerous criminal organization in the world. "In the past few decades, when every other social institution in America has either been shattered or changed forever, the Mafia has continued to thrive," write the authors of *Goombata*, a 1992 book on Gambino crime family leader John Gotti. "Like a virulent parasite, it has adapted to the host body, fastening on to whatever the law or social convention allowed."[7]

A direct descendent of the Sicilian organization transformed by U.S. mores and modern corporate methods, the American Mafia is a coalition of twenty-four separate groups (each known as a "family") who reside mainly in New York. Families are composed of "made men" (those sworn into the family, probably no more than 2,000 in the United States) and "associates" (those who work actively with the Mafia but have not been sworn in). In the early 1990s, law enforcement estimated La Cosa Nostra's annual income at $60 to $100 billion.[8]

Examination of the industry's distribution structure has led many to believe that organized porn is another facet of organized crime. For instance, the Organized Crime Division of the Washington, D.C., Police Department said in 1978,

> The pornography industry is characterized by a vertical distribution and a pyramid structure with a limited number of documented distributors within individual states. Porn is initially supplied to national distributors who then sell to inter-state distributors who in turn distribute to intra-state distributors.
>
> This limited number of pornography distributors may indicate the lucrative profits in the distributorship and production of porn with the capability of dictating prices to independent bookstore owners. As an example of high profits . . . a magazine can be produced for approximately fifty cents; wholesaled for five dollars and retailed for ten dollars. This computes to a 1900% profit production to consumer sale. In general, there is no competition or price wars, which indicates price control.[9]

The same report revealed the methods used by the Mafia's pornographers to avoid detection by law enforcement:

1. Names of corporate officers are used without the individual's knowledge or consent.
2. Notary publics are employed to notarize signatures without confrontation of signees (i.e., signatures of dubious origin are declared genuine, when they may in fact be forgeries).
3. Rubber stamps of signatures are used without the owner's knowledge.
4. Corporate names are constantly changed.
5. Controllers do not appear on corporate papers but are major stockholders.
6. Pornography entrepreneurs appear as corporate officers for a legitimate business that may have pornography distributors as subsidiaries.[10]

A major source of revenue for the Mafia is the sex trade, of which porn is a major component. New York's Colombo family, for instance, led organized crime into porn in the late 1960s, largely operating out of Times Square. The Colombos eventually earned millions of dollars from the 1972 porno movie *Deep Throat*, produced by Anthony Peraino.[11]

Peraino's family emerged out of the bloody Brooklyn gang bang of 1931 known as the Castellammarese War. Taking its name from one of the factions—immigrants from the town of Castellamare del Golfo in Sicily—the Mafia's first great power struggle in America brought to power such legendary mobsters as Lucky Luciano and Vito Genovese. Among those who died was Giuseppe Peraino, a member of the Profaci crime family, which became part of the Colombo family.[12]

Giuseppe left a wife, Grazia, and two sons, Anthony, 16, and Joseph, 5, who later produced and distributed the most profitable film of all time—*Deep Throat*. In the same year that his father died, Anthony was charged with murder. As with his next six arrests, Anthony escaped conviction. Law enforcement considered him and his brother Joseph "made" members of the Colombo crime family.[13]

Anthony jumped in at the start of the burgeoning porn business, which became organized crime's biggest new money-maker since the 1950s. Since the early 1970s, pornographers have grossed at least a billion dollars a year. Law enforcement estimates the Mafia's take as about half, making it the third biggest earner overall, following gambling and narcotics.[14]

In the late 1960s, Colombo member John "Sonny" Franzese began supplying 8mm hardcore stag movies to the coin-operated peep show machines in sex shops around New York's Time Square. The Colombo family soon controlled its own plant for processing 8mm movies—All-State Film Labs in Brooklyn. Anthony Peraino's son, Louis "Butchie" Peraino, officially owned the lab but a capo (lieutenant) in the Bonnano crime family, Michael Zaffarano (aka Mickey Z.), ran All-State's porn operations.[15]

Zaffarano and Peraino dominated distribution of loops to Mafia controlled outlets in New York City. According to the FBI, they sold their films secretly out of automobile trunks, coffee catering trucks, unmarked warehouses, several restaurants, a chain of meat markets, and a Brooklyn candy store.[16]

Louis Peraino entered the legitimate movie business through All-State Film Labs, presiding over Bryanston Distributors in its Hollywood heyday. Law enforcement investigators consider Louis, along with his older brother, Joseph S. Peraino, a Colombo family "associate" rather than a "made" member. One veteran investigator echoes the consensus among his peers when he says of Louis, "His grandfather was in organized crime, his father is in it, his uncle is in it, his brother is in it, so he's in it. That's the way it is. You don't get out."[17]

That "You don't get out" theme flows through the romantic *Godfather* saga, the book and movies that define the Mafia in the minds of millions. Many of those interviewed by the *Los Angeles Times* for its 1982 piece on the Perainos described Louis as a Michael Corleone figure—the brightest of the Peraino men and one who is driven by a desire for respectability.

"There is nothing ominous about Butchie Peraino," says movie producer Frank Avianca. "He's a big teddy bear."[18] Peraino financed and distributed Avianca's 1975 movie *The Human Factor*, and Sandy Howard's *The Devil's Rain* and *Echoes of Summer*. "Lou wanted to make an image for himself as a decent man," says Howard. "He tried to build a legitimate business."[19]

Porn star Linda Lovelace gives a different picture of Butchie in her 1980 bestseller, *Ordeal*. Louis was "heavy and sloppy. . . . What I remember most about him was his loud mouth. He was always yelling at somebody about something. And he never went anywhere without his bodyguard, Vinnie."[20]

Be he obnoxious or charming, Louis Peraino, along with his father, Anthony, and Uncle Joseph, became rich quick with the success of *Deep Throat*. The Perainos used the profits to build a vast financial empire, ranging from garment companies in New York to porn theaters in Los Angeles to drug smuggling in the Caribbean.[21]

As *Deep Throat* money poured into organized crime through the Perainos, the Mob increased its infiltration of the porn business. During the mid-1970s, they engaged in extortion and violence to control independent pornographers. A report by the Administrative Vice Division of the Los Angeles Police Department estimated that by 1976 organized crime controlled 80 percent of the Los Angeles–based porno movie production and distribution business. "Organized crime families from Chicago, New York, New Jersey, and Florida are openly controlling and directing the major pornography operations in Los Angeles."[22]

An investigative report submitted to the California legislature by the Attorney General of California discussed organized crime infiltration into the pornography industry:

> In the early 1970s . . . four organized crime groups moved in on pornography operations in California. They met relatively little resistance because the weak-structured organized crime group of Southern California lacked the strength to deter the infiltration of organized crime from the East.
>
> Organized crime figures first focused on production and retail operations in California. In this effort, they established national distribution networks and effectively resorted to illegal and unfair business tactics. [They] . . . illegally duplicated the films of independent producers and displayed them at nationwide organized crime controlled theaters. Faced with continued piracy and lost profits, many legitimate producers were forced to deal with organized crime controlled distribution companies and film processing labs.
>
> After gaining control of many wholesale and retail companies, organized crime forced other independent retailers out of business through price manipulation. Wholesale prices to independent retailers were raised while prices to organized crime controlled outlets were lowered. Independents were undersold . . . until lost profits forced them out of business. Many competitors were bought out which allowed the subsequent raising of prices in other parts of the market.[23]

A 1975 LAPD memo said that the success of *Deep Throat* prompted a large migration of major New York Mob figures to Los Angeles. The report warned that, once established in porn, the Mob's next logical move would be into the legitimate Hollywood movie business. And that's what happened.[24]

In September 1973, a Hollywood showbiz paper announced that "two New York businessmen" named Louis and Joseph Peraino had established "a major new film production and distribution company" called Bryanston, with plans for making "at least 10 feature motion pictures within the next year." The Perainos established Bryanston in July 1971, shortly after creating Damiano Film Productions. The two were "twin companies engaged in the financing, acquisition, production and distribution of motion picture film products of every kind, nature and gauge," according to a joint company prospectus that Louis Peraino prepared for a New York bank.[25] Damiano made porn while Bryanston went legit.

One of the first movies that Bryanston financed and produced in-house (for $600,000) was *The Last Porno Flick*, released in August 1974 as *The Mad, Mad Moviemakers*. In the film, two cab-driving buddies raise $22,000 to make a porno by telling their Italian family and friends they're making a religious movie. Complications arise when the porno becomes a hit. The film, which bombed, also features a Brando-esque Mafia boss. *The Last Porno Flick* pokes fun at the Perainos' experience with *Deep Throat*, which cost them $22,000 to make.

As Louis Peraino took his share of porn profits and turned his attention to mainstream movies in 1973, father Anthony and uncle Joseph took over the distribution of *Deep Throat*, shifting the base of operations from New York to a network of companies in Miami. But Louis oversaw L.A.–area distribution of the porno even as he pursued success in Hollywood. One of his key *Deep Throat* reps was former Brooklynite Joseph (Junior) Torchio, described by one LAPD investigator as "the best-known trunk-buster [auto break-in artist] in New York."[26] In 1973, Torchio, despite, in some people's opinion, not having an IQ above room temperature, became Bryanston's director of finance.

Torchio first came to the attention of police in 1969 when, on March 14, he set up the shooting of Mafia associate Alfred Adorno. Torchio moved to Los Angeles later that year and set up a porn production company with William Amerson and Jacob (Jack) Molinas, described in a California Department of Justice report as a "con man, swindler, disbarred attorney and former pro basketball player [Fort Wayne Pistons]."[27] An All American at Columbia University in the 1950s, Molinas was convicted in 1963 as the "master fixer" in a point-shaving scandal that rocked college basketball in 1961.[28] After his release from prison in 1968, Molinas moved to Los Angeles and entered porn. He dealt with several known figures in organized crime, including Michael Zaffarano. Torchio and Molinas received loans of $250,000 from Louis Peraino in 1973 and 1974, on which they later defaulted. With partner Bernard Gussoff, Molinas used his money to set up a fur importing company called Berjac as a front for distributing porn.[29]

In September 1974, Bryanston filed a lawsuit against Molinas for nonpayment of the loan. Two months later, Gussoff was beaten to death in his Los Angeles apartment. The murder was never solved. Less than a year later, in August 1975, Molinas was shot and killed as he stood in the backyard of his Hollywood Hills home. Three weeks later, Torchio, a day before he was scheduled to talk to the feds, was struck by a car and killed on the Las Vegas strip. All three murders appeared to be Mob hits.[30]

In 1974, trade papers like *Daily Variety* heralded Louis Peraino's Bryanston as the hottest independent distribution company in the motion picture industry. In October 1974 the company rode a crest of hits: *Andy Warhol's Frankenstein*, *Return of the Dragon*, and *The Texas Chainsaw Massacre*. With *Chainsaw* and *Deep Throat*, Louis produced the sex and violence trendsetters of the late twentieth century.

Director Tobe Hooper, who made *The Texas Chainsaw Massacre* and *Poltergeist,* begged off a *Los Angeles Times* interview about the Perainos and Bryanston. "All I know is that about two months after *Chainsaw* was released, I heard a rumor that Bryanston was a Mafia operation. . . . If these guys are behind door No. 1, then who's behind door No. 2 or door No. 3?"[31] Despite such common fears, other moviemakers describe Louis Peraino—who was arrested in Brooklyn in 1971 for chasing his wife down the street with a gun—as a warm family man.[32]

In a 1976 confidential memo, the California Department of Justice placed Bryanston at the top of a list of "key corporations," believed to be "controlled" by the Mob. "It appears that Bryanston coordinates the nationwide distribution of full-length films for organized crime."[33]

Not only does Hollywood like the Mafia, but the Mafia likes Hollywood. Show biz is not only fun, it's a great way to launder money. Most moviemakers will do anything to get financing for their projects and couldn't care less about using proceeds from drugs. Because the law requires reports to the IRS on all cash transactions in excess of $10,000, the immense profits of organized crime cannot be deposited in a bank. Instead, criminals clean their money by passing it through legitimate cash businesses like bars, parking lots, newsstands, and movie companies. For instance, a newsstand could claim that it did $85,000 business one day when it reality it only did $2,000. That way $83,000 of cash earned through activities such as drug sales can be brought into the legitimate economy.

An FBI agent told the *Los Angeles Times* that Hollywood doesn't care about dirty money.

> You are faced with a situation where there is a community acceptance of a set of standards that might be offensive in some areas,

but not here. And we have to look at it that way, just like we look at pornography, based on community standards. Unfortunately, we have a set of standards about how to finance motion pictures in Hollywood that is incredibly lax.

In the last ten years or so, we've made six or seven efforts to try to ferret our allegations of organized crime in the movie business. And we got zero support from the industry. They don't view it as a threat. It's good money to them. It's a way of life, condoned, even embraced. Nobody wants to expose it.[34]

The Perainos distributed *Deep Throat* between 1973 and 1976, using "checkers" and "sweepers" who traveled the country changing aliases and meeting secretly in hotel rooms and public restrooms to exchange information and cash. "Checkers" carried *Deep Throat* across state lines to adult theaters. Peraino's reps then stayed on to count the number of customers (i.e., people in the audience) and, at the end of the day's showings, collect their share of the take, usually half. "Sweepers" moved from checker to checker collecting money and shipping it or carrying it back to company offices in New Jersey and Florida. Federal agents shadowed them, as they had all of the Perainos' porn operations since 1969 [35]

In August 1974, a federal grand jury in Memphis indicted Louis Peraino, along with his father, Anthony, and uncle, Joseph, on charges of transporting obscene materials (*Deep Throat*) across state lines. Damiano Film Productions also was indicted but not Gerard Damiano himself, for he no longer held an interest in either *Deep Throat* or the production company.

In an October 1975 article in the *New York Times*, Nicholas Gage reported that Damiano sold his interest in the movie to Louis Peraino in July 1972 for $25,000. When a reporter commented to Damiano that he'd received a lousy deal, Damiano replied, "I can't talk about it." When the reporter persisted, Damiano said, "You want me to get both my legs broken?"[36]

Elsewhere in his front page article, Gage described brothers Anthony and Joseph S. Peraino as the "most successful of all Mafia figures involved in the production and distribution of hardcore films."

A day later, a similar report published in the *New York Post*, headlined "How the Mob Moved into Times Square" linked Louis Peraino to the Mafia, identifying him as a "reputed" member of the Colombo crime family.[37]

Former Bryanston publicist Patty Zimmerman says that the company's Beverly Hills office didn't receive a single inquiry from the West Coast media following the New York articles. Nor did the articles cause a stir among Bryanston employees.[38]

Two months later, *Variety* published a long and upbeat report on Bryanston, making no mention of *Deep Throat*, an upcoming trial in Memphis on charges of obscenity, or the New York newspaper allegations. The gushing coverage peaked in January 1976 in a *Variety* article headlined "Bryanston Expanding Its Operations": "The Bryanston operation is seeking out producers and talent who may have the idea but lack either the capital the deal. Company appears willing to look at anything beyond the fringe and take chances accordingly."[39]

On March 1, 1976, Anthony, Joseph, and Louis Peraino went on trial in Memphis along with Harry Reems and eight other defendants. Prosecutor Larry Parrish, an assistant district attorney, put together his case with help from the FBI, the IRS, and the U.S. Justice Department organized-crime strike forces in Brooklyn and Miami.

The government spent a million dollars to protect the moral standards of the citizens of Memphis, or so it seemed. But Bruce Kahmer, the attorney who represented Harry Reems in the case, says that "it wasn't an obscenity trial at all—it was a racketeering and tax evasion trial."[40] Adding strength to this argument was the job Parrish took after the trial—he ran the Brooklyn Strike Force, which only investigates organized crime.

Only introducing a handful of "expert" witnesses who proclaimed *Deep Throat* "obscene," the prosecutor spent most of the trial describing how *Deep Throat*'s distribution system worked. Parrish called more than fifty witnesses who'd worked for the Perainos. He supplemented the testimony with charts and graphs of the operation, leading the jury through the maze step by step. Defense attorneys offered little opposition to the government's description. Instead, they concentrated on the issue of the movie's supposed obscenity.

The prosecution showed that after the film's New York debut in June 1972, the Perainos distributed *Deep Throat* in the regular fashion through shipping prints to theaters by U.S. Mail and parcel post. Even though it was a federal crime to transport an obscene movie across state lines, the risk of prosecution seemed slight because the law contained no precise definition of obscenity. But this changed dramatically in June 1973, when the U.S. Supreme Court handed down its landmark "community standards" decision on pornography in *Marvin Miller* v. *California*.

In a five-to-four decision, the High Court removed from the language of the law the phrase "utterly without redeeming social value" which had long been the favorite loophole for pornographers. As a result of the new law, any prosecutor wishing to ban a sexual work no longer had to prove that it was "utterly without" value; it merely had to be lacking in "serious literary, artistic, political or scientific value" to be considered obscene. Now "community standards" instead of "national standards" ruled First Amendment obscenity cases.

This meant that magazines like *Playboy* and *Penthouse* or films like *Last Tango in Paris* might be banned in towns with conservative sexual values.

Pornographers could no longer justify their obscene works by reprinting on the flyleaf of their tawdry books a quotation of Voltaire, declared Chief Justice Warren Burger. "Conduct or depictions of conduct that the state police . . . can prohibit on a public street does not become automatically protected by the Constitution merely because the conduct is moved to a bar or a 'live' theatre stage, any more than a 'live' performance of a man and woman locked in a sexual embrace at high noon in Times Square is protected by the Constitution because they simultaneously engage in a valid political dialogue."[41]

A few days after the *Miller* ruling, police in Salt Lake City closed a theater showing *Last Tango in Paris.* Jack Valenti, president of the Motion Picture Association of America, said that it was now impossible to determine in advance whether a film violated obscenity law because the Supreme Court's ruling created "50 or more fragmented opinions as to what constituted obscenity."[42] The *New York Times* wrote that *Miller* gave "license to local censors. In the long run it will make every local community and every state the arbiter of acceptability, thereby adjusting all sex-related literary, artistic and entertainment production to the lowest common denominator of toleration. Police-court morality will have a heyday."[43]

In Hollywood, two studios negotiating to film Hubert Selby's book about working-class homosexuals, *Last Exit to Brooklyn*, abandoned the project. Art directors for *Playboy*, *Screw*, and other sex publications quickly modified their front covers. Customers at adult bookstores across the country stood in line to buy merchandise they feared would soon be banished from the shelves.[44]

"The immediate effect of this decision," said Bob Guccione of *Penthouse*, "will be to drive a multibillion-dollar industry underground—and that means graft and crime in the real sense. It's the same thing as a return to prohibition."[45]

After *Miller*, pornographers who lacked the money to pay attorneys got out of the business. "*Miller* made it all but impossible to distribute a film across state lines," says pioneering San Francisco pornographer Arlene Elster. "I knew the films would never get better if you couldn't distribute them, so I gave up and got out."[46]

The *Miller* decision was bad news for the distributors of *Deep Throat* because it meant that they were vulnerable to federal prosecution based on the most blue-nosed views of any Bible-belt township. So the Perainos developed a new distribution system to confound the feds. Those who didn't cooperate received threats of physical harm.

Other producers and distributors restricted the venues in which their films played. Jim and Artie Mitchell originally confined *Behind the Green Door* to a handful of theaters because they feared harassment from the FBI and the justice department. While getting busted for obscenity in a city like San Francisco was a hassle, what producers mainly feared were the feds. If a California pornographer was convicted of showing an obscene film in a place like Cincinnati, which, after *Miller*, was more likely, and if the feds could prove the person shipped the film over state lines, the pornographer was in trouble. Defending cases in federal court takes more time and money, and the penalties are more severe.[47]

With people standing in line to see *Deep Throat*, *The Devil in Miss Jones*, and *Behind the Green Door*, the Mafia recognized an opportunity. Through their organization they could distribute films under the table, taking the heat off producers, or they could copy the film and distribute it themselves. In 1973, Robert De Salvo and James Bochis, representatives for godfather Carlo Gambino, tried for the rights to *Behind the Green Door.* They told Jim and Artie Mitchell that they could share the profits of national distribution of *Green Door* 50/50 or the Mafia would simply steal the prints to the movie and cut the Mitchells out of the money altogether. The brothers refused the offer. A few weeks later they discovered that Gambino had made hundreds of pirated versions of the movie, scooping off the cream of the market.[48]

On April 30, 1976, the Memphis jury found the Perainos and all other defendants guilty on conspiring to distribute obscenity across state lines. Louis and his uncle Joseph S. Peraino received one-year prison sentences and fines of $10,000. The judge delayed sentencing of Anthony Peraino until his capture. (He had fled to Europe to escape the trial.)[49]

A month after the trial, Bryanston closed up its West Coast office and disappeared as quickly as it had come, leaving behind a score of puzzled employees and a trail of debt. In addition to nearly $750,000 in taxes, the company owed undetermined millions throughout the movie marketplace. In August 1976, Louis Peraino made his last public statement, published in the pages of *Variety*, to the movie industry: "Don't worry about it. I can't say more now . . . but I'll be back in business."[50]

Louis returned to showbiz in September 1977, lending $50,000 to the owner of a Los Angeles–based music company in return for a 40 percent interest. Two weeks later, according to the Los Angeles Police Department, Peraino showed up at the music company office carrying an envelope which contained a revolver and a document naming Peraino sole owner of the company. Louis put the envelope on the desk. Upon seeing it, a partner signed the document and went into hiding.[51]

Peraino's $50,000 loan was in the form of a check, which eventually bounced, drawn on a bank in Panama. But Peraino had taken over the company and milked it for cash before moving on.

In 1978, Joseph and Louis Peraino established Arrow Film & Video with offices in New York City and Van Nuys, California. An LAPD officer, Sgt. Joseph Ganley, testified in the FBI's MIPORN case (short for Miami Pornography, the FBI's biggest investigation of porn) that Louis Peraino on two occasions in 1979 threatened the owners of Los Angeles–area porn film companies with "bodily harm" if they continued to reproduce and sell prints of *Deep Throat* without paying the royalties he demanded.[52]

❖❖❖❖

While the Perainos made the highest grossing porno ever, the world's dominant pornographer during the early 1970s was Michael Thevis, who owned about 40 percent of the nation's smut business with an annual take of $100 million.[53] He controlled more than 400 bookstores and theaters in the southeast United States through bombings, arson, extortion, and murder.[54]

Born in Raleigh, North Carolina, in 1932, Thevis was raised in the Greek Orthodox Church by strict immigrant grandparents. While other boys played games, Mike worked, for he was taught that toil, education, and success were a natural order of life.

Lack of money forced Thevis to drop out of college and take a job in downtown Atlanta as a $50-a-week employee in a newsstand. Eventually, by the 1960s, he owned a string of stands. Frustrated by his inability to provide for his family (Thevis was married and had three children), he began offering pornographic materials at his newsstands, expanding from publications such as *Playboy* and *Oui* to magazines and films featuring bondage, bestiality, and child porn. Thevis worked closely with Robert DiBernardo, named in various law enforcement reports as a member of the DeCavalcante and the Gambino crime families. "Don't forget, Mike," a police wire-tap recorded DiBernardo as saying when Thevis boasted he owned 90 percent of America's peep shows, "you manage the machines. The family is in charge."[55]

Career criminal Roger Dean Underhill met Thevis in the fall of 1967 and together they developed a profitable peep show machine that was manufactured and distributed by two Thevis-controlled corporations, Automatic Enterprises and Cinematics. Underwood and Thevis set fire to competitors' buildings and even murdered a fellow Atlanta pornographer in November 1970. A couple of years later, they knocked off an employee who complained about his wages.[56]

After betting paroled in January 1977, Underhill turned FBI informant in exchange for immunity for his crimes. Due in part to his assistance, prosecutors put together an airtight case of racketeering against Thevis. Before the information could be given to a federal grand jury, however, on April 28, 1978, Thevis escaped from jail and had Underhill murdered. Thevis was arrested and confined to a federal prison in Danbury, Connecticut, where he confessed his crime to a cellmate. On October 26, 1979, Thevis was sentenced to life in prison for conspiring to murder Underhill and he received an extra twenty years for using murder and arson in a pattern of racketeering.[57]

Thevis remains in jail. His ex-wife, sons, and former secretary Laverne Bowden are thought to control many of the pieces of his former empire. Through the mid-1990s, consumers in the southeastern United States found it almost impossible to get porn. No other pornographer in the area had the resources or gumption to fight the feds and district attorneys who were bent on shutting down the industry.

❖❖❖❖

The successor to Thevis as the world's most powerful pornographer, Reuben Sturman, came to dominate porn during the 1980s as much as Bill Gates dominates computers in the 1990s. And Sturman achieved his success despite constant harassment by the federal government. In 1964, FBI agents raided Sturman's Cleveland warehouse and seized 590 copies of a paperback called *Sex Life of a Cop*. Sturman responded to his indictment on federal obscenity charges by suing the head of the FBI, J. Edgar Hoover. Eventually the charges against Sturman (and Hoover) were dismissed, but for the next two decades, state, local, and federal officials constantly raided Sturman's warehouses. Indicted on federal obscenity charges four more times during these years, Sturman avoided conviction on every count and never spent a day in prison. Like crime leader John Gotti, the porn king's stature increased with each victory over the federal government.[58]

Sturman created porn companies in England, France, Switzerland, Germany, and the Netherlands. He opened factories in Asia to make sex toys such as dildos and vibrators. As early as 1974, Sturman, like Mafia don Carlo Gambino, recognized that the future of porn lay in videotape. He put his films on video, opened retail video stores, and began distributing hardcore videos in the United States and western Europe. Sturman commanded 800 adult bookstores in all fifty states and forty foreign countries and a chain of peep shows under the name of Western Amusements. He manufactured his own peep machines (Automatic Vending), provided lie-detector tests for employee security (National Polygraph), and distributed sex toys under the trade name Doc Johnson (Marche Manufacturing).[59]

During the 1970s, Sturman opened up porn distribution centers in most of America's largest cities. His first was Cuyahoga News, but as his empire grew, Sturman thought more grandly. He founded Sovereign News, then Royal News, Castle, Noble, and Crown. Sturman came to regard his choice of names as a mistake, for their similarity enabled the government to trace his network more easily.

An Internal Revenue Service agent who spent most of his adult life investigating Reuben Sturman finally put the porn king behind bars in 1992. In 1975, at age twenty-seven, Richard N. Rossfelder Jr. began investigating Sturman because he suspected that the Cleveland pornographer used his elaborate corporate structure to avoid taxes. He was right. Sturman skimmed millions of dollars from his peep show machines each year and hid the money in offshore accounts.[60]

After years of detective work, Rossfelder tracked down Sturman's Swiss bank accounts, and in an unprecedented move, the Swiss government gave the IRS access to them after the U.S. Justice Department handed over secret documents linking Sturman with such organized crime families as the Gambinos of New York and the DeCavalcantes in New Jersey.[61]

Sturman delayed his tax trial until 1989 by challenging the legality of the Justice Department's actions, demanding to see the secret documents and denying any connection with the Mafia. The pornographer used the extra time to verbally sell off his empire to family (such as his eldest son, David, who received General Video West, the dominant distributor on the West Coast) and friends (like Edward Wedelstedt, who gained control of hundreds of Sturman's sex shops).[62]

In 1989, Reuben and David Sturman were found guilty of tax evasion. In exchange for testifying against his father,

David served only two years. Reuben was sentenced to four years after a plea bargain with the Justice Department.

While serving his sentence, Sturman became angry that operators of twelve of his bookstores failed to kickback to him as verbally agreed. For example, when the owner of Phoenix's sex shop Pleasure World died in 1990, his widow took over the business. She noticed that monthly payments of $1,000 had been made to someone named Reuben Sturman but she could find no bill or contract to justify them. So she stopped paying. Sturman called her to explain the arrangement but she ignored him. Around Thanksgiving 1991, Sturman arranged for thugs to smash the store's video machines. The payments resumed.[63]

Paula Lawrence and Roy May, owners of several Chicago sex shops, supposedly owed Reuben about $100,000 a month. Sturman had sold the stores to them in a verbal agreement for $35,000 a month and 2 percent of the gross sales. With Sturman incarcerated, the operators made payments to the IRS instead of Reuben.[64]

Getting help from Herbert Feinberg, aka Mickey Fine, Sturman hired outlaw bikers from California to smash eight porn shops in Chicago and four in Milwaukee as "payment overdue" warnings. Taking plastic explosives on board their plane, the bikers flew to Chicago, where they drove in two different vehicles to blow up a selected store. Stray electronic signals from a traffic light accidentally ignited a bomb in one car, killing one thug and injuring another. The survivor became a witness for the government against Sturman, who realized that he was going to be convicted of the bombing conspiracy.[65]

To avoid the new charges, Sturman escaped from his minimum security prison on the night of December 7, 1992, with the aid of a helicopter, disappearing into the Mojave

Desert. Federal officials assumed he'd fled the country and would never be seen again. Eight weeks later, however, he was found in an apartment near Disneyland.

Within a month of his recapture, Sturman was indicted and accused of hiring men to damage and destroy peep show booths at bookstores in Cleveland, Chicago, and Phoenix. The jury acquitted him of the bombings, but convicted him of conspiring to commit extortion through the use of violence. After deliberating less than two hours, a federal jury in 1994 convicted Herbert "Mickey" Feinberg of attempted murder through his hiring of four men to bomb the sex shops.[66]

Because Sturman owed $29 million in back taxes, the IRS seized all his available assets. "This was the biggest case the IRS criminal division had ever seen," says Rossfelder. "Its effect on the rest of the porn industry was monumental. There were a lot of people in this industry reporting nickels and dimes who now report hundreds of thousands of dollars."[67]

In September 1995, a mysterious fire virtually leveled the Doc Johnson sex toy plant in North Hollywood, which was formerly owned by Sturman. Then someone blew up a bank in the Cayman Islands. Law enforcement speculates that the two events amounted to a last battle for control of Sturman's remaining empire. According to insiders, three major factions fought for control of the porn industry, and the Cayman Islands bombing targeted a place where a significant amount of one of the faction's assets resided. The bombing concluded the struggle, and the three groups—one of them headquartered in Paris—agreed to divide the international porn market into equal shares.[68]

In late 1997, Sturman died of a massive heart attack.

After Thevis and Sturman, the third porn mogul of the 1970s was Harry Virgil Mohney of Durand, Michigan. He imported large quantities of Euro-porn and controlled about sixty adult bookstores; a string of massage parlors, X-rated theaters, and drive-in movies; go-go joints; and a topless billiards hall. Sharing Reuben Sturman's passion for privacy, Mohney "has a working relationship with DeCavalcante representative Robert DiBernardo," according to a 1979 Department of Justice report, "and has met with Vito Giacalone and Joseph Zerilli of the LCN [La Cosa Nostra] Detroit. He has to cater to both to operate in Michigan."[69]

After his 1977 divorce, Mohney took eighteen-year-old Gail Palmer, who received "director" credit for eleven leading porn movies, including the *Candy* series starring Carol Connors, as his mistress. When Palmer eventually split from Mohney, she told authorities about his tax evasion. At the same time, an investigation of a New Year's Day fire in Indianapolis uncovered documents that led to a search of Mohney's Michigan warehouse. Agents learned that Mohney ran more than seventy corporations and skimmed more than $1 million a year from just one of them.[70]

❖❖❖❖

Chicago produced little pornography but consumed tons. The largest distributor was Capitol News Agency owned by Reuben Sturman and operated by Neil Traynor. Capitol controlled 80 percent of the distribution of porn magazines and films in Chicago.[71]

Since before the days of Al Capone, Chicago has hosted murderously aggressive mob families. Midwestern hoodlums muscled their way into the burgeoning sex business in the 1970s through extortion, arson, bombings, and murder. The

Gambino, Colombo, Bonanno-Galante, and the DeCaval-
cante Mob families ran the show with help from locals
Michael Glitta, Anthony DeFalco, Joseph "Doves" Aiuppa,
Gus Alex, James "Turk" Torello, and the Anthony "Big
Tuna" Accardo family.[72]

The Mafia exacted 50 percent tribute from Chicago's sex
shops, verified by frequent trips to the accounting books.
Two partners who refused to submit received threats followed up by violence. Thugs tossed a pipe bomb through the
window of one of their bookstores, and firebombed a porn
distribution center. Chicago's smut merchants promptly fell
into line.[73]

"What the speakeasies were during Prohibition," writes
Clifford L. Linedecker in his 1981 book, *Children in Chains*,
"porno is today. It is a product for which there is a
demanding market, it is handled by cash sales, and to a large
extent it is clandestine. Undertakings closed to public
scrutiny allow crime to breed much more easily than those
open to inspection and control. But the pornography trade
attracts stubborn, determined men. Some of them are willing
to fight and put their lives on the line."[74]

One such example is Paul Gonsky, who, after losing thousands of dollars providing art films, switched to porn. Gonsky
bought six theaters in Chicago and Indiana, earning money
and enemies in the Mob, who firebombed three of his theaters. A competing company operated by a cousin of Mafia
boss Phil Alderiso opened a new X-rated theater a few blocks
from one of the theaters operated by Gonsky. On the night
the new movie house opened, a bomb blew away the
entrance to Gonsky's theater.

Around noon on a crisp September day in 1977, Gonsky
was found lying on the ground in a parking lot near one of
his theaters in Old Town, a three-block-long corridor of bars,

arcades, head shops, and strip joints. Seven bullets had smashed into his body, shattering his head.

The murder was never solved and no Mafia connection was ever proven, because among the problems investigators face with the violence associated with commercial sex in America is the reluctance of victims and witnesses to talk. People who deal with the Mafia learn to keep their mouths shut. Several came under police scrutiny, however, including mob enforcer Frank Schweihs, pornographer Patrick "Patsy" Ricciardi, and Gonsky's partner Steven Hal Toushin. Toushin had been taken to court by Gonsky and another partner, Jeffrey Begun, for funneling money from their business into his own pockets. Begun understood the Gonsky assassination as a message and fled to California. Bereft of partners, Toushin took over the Chicago porn operation by default.[75]

To combat the Mafia's porn racket, in 1977 the FBI launched MIPORN, its most concerted investigation of the industry. (Recall that, as was mentioned previously, MIPORN is an acronym derived from the location of FBI front operations, "Miami," and the subject of the investigation, "pornography.") Two FBI agents, Bruce Ellavsky and Patrick Livingston, moved to Miami in September 1977. Operating out of a warehouse, they posed as a pair of sleazy porno film buyers for a company they set up called Golde Coaste Specialties. The agents later set up G&C Sales, Ltd., in the Grand Cayman Islands, to lend credibility to the operation.[76]

Bruce Ellavsky, tall and handsome, used the undercover name Bruce Wakerly and Patrick Livingstone, short and balding, became Pat Salamone. For thirty weeks, Ellavsky and Livingstone wore open-necked shirts, sported gold chains and diamond pinky rings, and drove around in rented Cadillacs, sometimes with a pair of beautiful women hanging on their arms. The agents infiltrated the porn industry and dealt with top crime figures who pirated mainstream movies as well as produced and distributed smut.

Because such theft cost Hollywood a billion dollars a year, mainstream distributors contributed much of MIPORN's $300,000 budget which funded the FBI agents' trips to pornographers and mobsters in every major U.S. city, including New York, Los Angeles, San Francisco, Las Vegas, Chicago, Pittsburgh, Minneapolis, and Providence.

When the wiseguys became suspicious and the lives of the FBI investigators appeared in danger, the undercover agents stopped paying their bills, which helped establish their credibility. Ellavsky and Livingston eventually gained the confidence of inept Los Angeles pornographer Rubin Gottesman.

In April 1978, Ellavsky and Livingston attended a porn convention at the Fairmont Hotel in New Orleans, Louisiana. At a restaurant in the hotel, Gottesman introduced the agents to Teddy Rothstein, who agreed to supply Golde Coaste Specialties with 8mm hardcore films, magazines, and videotapes. Rothstein later introduced the undercover agents to his 8mm man, Andre D'Apice, who said the agents "would have no problem dealing with Mr. Rothstein or Dibi [Robert DiBernardo] as long as you are 100% good people. . . . But if you should cross Dibi there are plenty of people who would kill for him."[77]

The net was spread further in May 1978, when the agents met with Norman Arno, who owned S&L Distributors of Los Angeles. Arno said he dealt with Rubin Gottesman for pirated videocassette copies of mainstream motion pictures such as *Jaws*. In exchange for payment in cash for these pirated films, Arno offered to give the agents "phony" invoices. Arno insisted on receiving no calls concerning these illegally copied mainstream videotapes. Instead, he wanted to make arrangements whereby he'd call the agents from a pay telephone to get their orders. Arno said he'd been reluctant to tell the agents he dealt with pirated movies as this violated federal copyright statutes. He said that there'd been a lot of activity by the FBI recently and that several producers of pirated films had been "busted" and now worked for the FBI.[78]

In February 1979, the undercover agents asked Gottesman for a print of the 1978 porno classic *Debbie Does Dallas*, which Gottesman had seen the night before. The pornographer told them he wouldn't even consider doing this because he wanted to remain healthy. Gottesman said Michael Zaffarano, a former bodyguard for godfather Joseph Bonanno and an associate of strong man Carmine Galante, would not hesitate to use muscle if he believed someone was bootlegging his movies. On March 23, 1979, Gottesman told the agents that in the past an individual who'd pirated hardcore movies was "hit in the head."[79]

The undercover FBI agents found that each of the major Cosa Nostra crime families in New York maintained West Coast representatives. Robert DiBernardo represented the DeCavalcantes, Thomas Ricciardi the Colombos, and William Haimowitz (William Bittner) the Gambinos. Ricciardi worked frequently with L.A. pornographer William Noel Finc who operated Fine Films and Billy Fine Productions. Haimowitz was raised by Carlo Gambino's lieutenant Ettore Zappi and said that Zappi sent him to California to corner the porn market for the Gambino family.[80]

Michael Zaffarano, a captain in the crime family of Joseph Bonanno and Carmine Galante, operated J&G Sales and Miracle Film Releasing Corporation of Los Angeles with partners Stuart Charles Segall and Tommy Sinopoli—all of whom were associated with the DeCavalcante family in New Jersey.[81] Segall began his career in entertainment as a porn actor working for Ted Paramore, later becoming a director and producer. With Theodore Gaswirth and John Holmes's manager William Amerson, Segall owned Capricorn Industries in Beverly Hills.

Zaffarano served as president of Stu Segall Associates, which had offices in New York and Hollywood. During the 1970s, Zaffarano and Segall directed the nationwide Pussycat Cinema chain of adult theaters. In the 1990s, Segall became a powerful producer of mainstream entertainment, including the TV show *Renegade*.

Mafiosi like Zaffarano, as a rule, don't run businesses, because the Mob generally contents itself with a piece of the action. According to Jeremiah B. McKenna, general counsel to the New York State Select Committee on Crime, the Mob's main interest in the New York sex business expresses itself through real estate deals. The Mafia leases buildings for ten years from legitimate owners and then subleases them to the fly-by-night operators of massage parlors, sex shops, and peep shows, at $110 to $130 a day cash—double what other businesses would pay. "The shops close up and move on, but that lease stays there until the next fly-by-nighter comes along. The property is held for the sex industry," McKenna said. "A guy can't come in and start selling shoes because the money is too great."[82]

After eighteen months of the MIPORN investigation, the FBI decided to act. On Valentine's Day, 1979, at noon, 400 FBI agents swept into porno movie theaters, warehouses, retail stores, and offices in thirteen major U.S. cities, arresting many of the biggest names in porn on federal obscenity and racketeering charges. Among the fifty-eight persons arrested (thirty-three from California) were brothers Louis and Joseph C. Peraino—rounded up in the New York office of their company Arrow Film & Video. They were charged with interstate shipment of obscenity in the form of hardcore videos titled *Candy Stripers*, *Liquid Lips*, *His Master's Touch*, and *Hollywood Cowboy*.

Michael Zaffarano was the one casualty of the operation. When officers arrived at his New York office, fifty-eight-year-old "Mickey Z." suffered a heart attack and died on the spot, clutching a reel of pornographic film that the officers presume he was trying to destroy. "We killed him for sure," said one policeman at the scene, "and we saved the taxpayers a lot of money."[83]

Zaffarano's death created a power vacuum in organized crime's now international porn operations, provoking fights among the main Mafia families for dominance of the sex trade. In November 1981, Joseph S. Peraino, then fifty-five years old and a member of the Colombo family, was wounded outside his Brooklyn home by men armed with 9mm handguns.

On January 4, 1982, Joseph's competitors struck again, chasing him and his thirty-one-year-old son, Joseph Jr., through Brooklyn. The pursued men screeched to a halt on Lake Street and ran up the stairs onto the front porch of a modest brick duplex. The Perainos pounded on the door seeking refuge until a barrage of gunfire cut them down. The father was seriously wounded in the buttocks and legs; the son was hit six times in the head and killed. An innocent bystander was also killed. As Peraino lay bleeding with his murdered son at his side, he refused to tell police who fired the shots, what kind of car they drove, or which way they had gone.[84]

For their 1981 convictions in the MIPORN case, Louis Peraino and Joseph C. Peraino received prison terms of six and three years, respectively. They were not charged with film piracy, even though police found more than fifty major Hollywood movies at their Arrow offices as well as equipment capable of reproducing them in quantity. The list of films confiscated included most of the box-office hits of the previous decade—*Animal House, Kramer vs. Kramer, The Sting, Star Wars,* and *The Godfather.*[85]

Looking tired and short of breath, Anthony Peraino was sentenced that same month to ten months in prison and $15,000 in fines for his original 1976 *Deep Throat* conviction and subsequent bail-jumping charge. After five years as a fugitive, the ailing Peraino family head had turned himself in to authorities in 1981.[86]

The shootings and convictions marked the end of the Perainos' dominance in porn. As part of their sentence, they were supposed to abstain from all dealings in the masturbation business.

Like Sturman and Mohney, veteran pornographer Ken Guarino was lucky to escape conviction in the MIPORN sweep. Beginning his porn career in his teens, the expert corporate shell shuffler spent his considerable talents creating dummy corporations and business spider webs to launder Mob money, avoid taxes, and set up large offshore savings accounts.[87] Majority owner of porn conglomerate South Pointe Enterprises Inc., the corporate parent of Metro Home Video, Guarino's company went public in 1994 "to become more acceptable" by buying an inactive corporate shell rather than using the traditional method of a public offering.[88]

Adult Video News gushed about the company's NASDAQ listing in its October 1994 issue: "No move in industry history; no television interview or personal appearance; no post-adult career of an actress or actor; no court victory; no business success or humanitarian gesture does more to promote the social and legal acceptance of adult entertainment than the simple act of placing South Pointe on the same legal and financial level as thousands of other public companies that provide jobs, make products and provide services to the consuming and investing public."[89]

In January 1997, Guarino and Natale Richichi pled guilty to charges of conspiracy to defraud the government. The government said in the Memoranda of Plea Agreement that, had the case gone to trial, evidence would have been presented proving that Richichi is a "capo in the Gambino crime family of Cosa Nostra" and that Guarino made "tribute payments" to Richichi for protection of his multimillion-dollar pornography empire against extortion attempts by other factions of the Mafia.[90]

> Unlike most [captains] who can only deal with the boss of their family through an adviser, and who would not be in a position to advise higher ranking members of other La Cosa Nostra families, Richichi has dealt directly with John Gotti. . . .
> . . . He has also been intercepted providing extensive advice to Frank Salemme Jr., the boss of the New England La Cosa Nostra family. Richichi is also known to be highly respected by other La Cosa Nostra families and (captains) of various La Cosa Nostra families who reside in the Vegas area appear to give Richichi deference as well.[91]

According to prosecutors, Guarino paid Natale Richichi, a confidante of John Gotti, and his son Salvatore $15,000 a month and laundered millions of dollars for them to prevent invasion of Guarino's porn empire, to get permission from the New England branch of Cosa Nostra to operate a precious metals business in the Northeast, and to use their influence with union officials for favorable treatment.[92]

In April 1997, Guarino was sentenced to sixteen months in federal prison and fined $250,000. His company, Metro, one of America's four biggest porn producers, gained fame in 1999 for hosting the "Houston 500," a five-hundred-man gangbang of porn star Houston.

❖❖❖❖

MIPORN prosecutors convicted forty-nine of the fifty-five charged pornographers, many of them (such as Chuck Bernstein, Russ Hampshire, and Walter Gernert) for dealing in illegally duplicated movies. The Mob forced the sale of pirated tapes through the video dealers they controlled. Movies such as *Superman II* made fortunes for the thieves who copied them and offered them for sale on tape. Another charge leveled was that since these criminals presumably controlled much of the videocassette distribution of adult films, they violently suppressed the pirating of their own films. Sources claim that at least fifty pornographers have been knocked off by the Mob since 1969.[93]

Notes

1. See, for example, U.S. Department of Justice, Attorney General's Commission on Pornography, Final Report, particularly pages 1040–1240 (Washington, D.C.: U.S. Government Printing Office, 1986), hereafter referred to as Meese Commission Report; Gary Potter, *The Porn Merchants* (Dubuque, Iowa: Kendall Hunt, 1986); Ellen Farley and William K. Knoedelseder Jr., *Los Angeles Times*, June 13, 20, and 27, 1982; Michael Satchell, "The Big Business of Selling Smut," *Parade* magazine, August 19, 1979; James Cook, "The X-Rated Economy," *Forbes*, September 18, 1978; Report by the Task Force on Organized Crime published by the Law Enforcement Assistance Administration as quoted in the Senate, Congressional Record, January 30, 1984, beginning on p. 845.

2. Meese Commission Report, p. 1040.

3. Ibid., pp. 1047–48.

4. Ibid., p. 1048.

5. Ibid., pp. 1048–49.

6. Ibid., p. 1071.

7. John Cummings and Ernest Volkman, *Goombata* (Boston: Little, Brown, 1992), p. 3.

8. Ibid., pp. 3–5.

9. "Organized Crime's Involvement in the Pornography Industry," Report of the Investigative Services Division, Metropolitan Police Dept., Washington, D.C. (1978). Quoted in the Meese Commission Report, p. 1207.

10. Ibid., 1208.

11. Farley and Knoedelseder, "The Pornbrokers," June 13, 1982.

12. Ibid.

13. Ibid.

14. Ibid.

15. Ibid.

16. Ibid.

17. Ibid.

18. Ibid.

19. Ibid.

20. Linda Lovelace with Mike McGrady, *Ordeal* (New York: Lyle Stuart, 1980), p. 119.

21. Farley and Knoedelseder, "The Pornbrokers," June 13, 1982; Meese Commission Report, p. 1052.

22. Investigative Report on Organized Crime and Pornography Submitted to the Attorney General of California (1977). Quoted in the Meese Commission Report, p. 1049.

23. Ibid.

24. Farley and Knoedelseder, "The Pornbrokers," June 13, 1982.

25. Ibid.

26. Ibid.

27. Ibid.

28. Ibid.

29. Ibid.

30. Ibid.

31. Ibid.

32. Ibid.

33. Farley and Knoedelseder, "The Pornbrokers," June 27, 1982.

34. Ibid.

35. Ibid.

36. Nicholas Gage, "Organized Crime Reaps Huge Profits from Dealing in Pornographic Films," *New York Times*, October 12, 1975, p. l:l.

37. Quoted by Farley and Knoedelseder, "The Pornbrokers," June 27, 1982.

38. Ibid.

39. Ibid.

40. Ibid.

41. Quoted by Gay Talese, *Thy Neighbor's Wife* (New York: Doubleday, 1980), p. 338.

42. Ibid., p. 339.

43. Ibid.

44. Ibid., p. 338.

45. Ibid., p. 340.

46. John Hubner, *Bottom Feeders* (New York: Doubleday, 1992), p. 208.

47. Ibid.

48. Ibid., p. 211.

49. Ibid., and Farley and Knoedelseder, "The Pornbrokers," June 27, 1982.

50. Farley and Knoedelseder, "The Pornbrokers," June 27, 1982.

51. Ibid.

52. Ibid.

53. Potter, *The Porn Merchants*, p. 107.

54. Ibid.; *United States* v. *Thevis*, 665 F.2d 616 (5th Cir.

1982); and John Heidenry, *What Wild Ecstasy* (New York: Simon & Schuster, 1997), pp. 231–33.

55. Cook, "The X-Rated Economy."

56. *United States* v. *Thevis.*

57. Ibid.

58. Eric Schlosser, "The Business of Pornography," *U.S. News & World Report* (February 10, 1997): 50.

59. Ibid., p. 51.

60. Ibid.

61. Ibid.

62. Heidenry, *What Wild Ecstasy*, pp. 319–20.

63. Ibid.

64. Ibid.

65. Ibid.

66. Ibid.

67. Schlosser, "The Business of Pornography."

68. Heidenry, *What Wild Ecstasy*, pp. 371–72.

69. Meese Commission Report, pp. 1230–36.

70. "King of Clubs," *Detroit News*, October 20, 1991, 1:1.

71. Clifford L. Linedecker, *Children in Chains* (New York: Everest House, 1981), p. 72.

72. Ibid., p. 73.

73. Ibid., p. 74.

74. Ibid.

75. Ibid., pp. 72–77.

76. Meese Commission Report, pp. 1072–75

77. Ibid., p. 1077.

78. Ibid., p. 1084.

79. Ibid., p. 1095.

80. Ibid., p. 1214.

81. Ibid., p. 1213.

82. "Neighborhood Porn Wars," *Newsday*, April 18, 1993.

83. Farley and Knoedelseder, "The Pornbrokers," June 13, 1982.

84. Ibid.

85. Ibid.

86. Ibid.

87. W. Zachary Malinowsky, "R.I. Pornographer Pleads Guilty," *Providence Journal-Bulletin*, January 11, 1997.

88. John R. Wilke, "Porn Broker," *Wall Street Journal*, July 11, 1994.

89. Jack Point, "Adult Goes Airborne," *Adult Video News* (October 1994).

90. Malinowsky, "R.I. Pornographer."

91. Ibid.

92. Ibid.

93. Meese Commission Report, p. 1095.

6.

Snuff Child Bestiality

*P*ornographers produced their best and worst films during the 1970s, experimenting with explicit depictions of bestiality, children, and rape. Out of control, they precipitated a backlash against the sex industry during the Reagan–Bush era.

"Everything moved so fast," pioneer Howard Ziehm told *Screw* magazine. "When things moved slowly, the public assimilated it. But when hardcore came in, it just went berserk. Within seven weeks, fucking and sucking wasn't enough; they wanted dog movies."[1]

The nastiest of all porno is the snuff film, which has two key elements—it must show real sex and murder (preferably at the point of the female's orgasm), and it must be commercially distributed. Despite wild rumors, not one snuff film has ever been proven to exist.

The origin of the myth of the snuff film dates to 1973 when Raymond Gauer, the president of an antipornography group, Citizens for Decency through Law, claimed porno films which climaxed with a woman being murdered were circulating. "I've never seen one," Gauer told *Adam* magazine, but "my undercover guy, though he's never seen one, has talked to enough people to be convinced they exist. Another source is convinced they exist in quantity, and that they've been screened in the very 'In' circles in Hollywood."[2] Gauer's remarks illustrate the greatest problem with snuff films—nobody has ever seen one but many know of somebody else's claim to have seen one.

The allegations played well with the media. Tabloid newspapers like the *New York Post* and the *Daily News* ran stories of the ongoing investigations by law enforcement with banner headlines like "Snuff Porn—The Actress Is Actually Killed."

As rumors ran wild, an enterprising film producer, Allen Shackleton, bought the rights to a 1970 low-budget film called *The Slaughter*, made by Michael and Roberta Findlay. The film was so bad that it was never released, but it was perfect for Shackleton's purpose since it was shot in Argentina. The tabloids said that snuff films came from South America. Allen added ten minutes of "reality" footage and retitled the film *Snuff*.

The extra few minutes show a woman on the crew telling the director how much she got turned on by the stabbing scene. So the director stabs her, slices off her fingers, cuts off her legs, rips open her abdomen, pulls out her intestines and holds them over his head. The film appears to run out as the screen goes black and a voice says, "Did you get it all?" "Yeah, we got it. Let's get out of here." No credits roll.

Shackleton never claimed that the snuff was real but allowed viewers to speculate. The New York City district attorney investigated the circumstances surrounding the making of the film and interviewed the actress who was supposedly murdered in the final segment. *Snuff* had a short run and few people remember it, but the idea that snuff films circulate still haunts the public imagination. In 1994, Rider McDowell, a reporter for the *San Francisco Chronicle*, spent six months trying to find a snuff film and failed.

The snuff film myth is particularly popular among feminists. "In these films, women actually were maimed, sliced to pieces, fucked, and killed," writes Andrea Dworkin.[3] In a 1993 book, *Only Words*, Catherine MacKinnon describes men who masturbate while watching women "mutilated, dismembered, bound, gagged, tortured and killed" and portrays snuff as "sexual murder in the process of being committed. Doing the murder is sex for those who do it. The climax is the moment of death."[4] Neither MacKinnon nor Dworkin cite any examples of snuff films, however.

After murder, the most evil deed that pornographers commit, at least in parts of the popular imagination, is screwing children. At the end of the twentieth century, mainstream pornographers, like the American industry trade group the Free Speech Coalition, proclaim that they have nothing to do with child porn. That's because they can no longer get away with it. When pornographers could deal in explicit materials featuring children, many did.

By the mid-1970s, child porn was available at sex shops in big cities like New York, Los Angeles, and Chicago. Most of the child pornography came from Europe, Asia, and North Africa. Many photos depicted erotic nudity rather than sex, and about 20 percent were pirated from nudist magazines, showing children at innocent play. The number of minors shown in commercial child pornography magazines and films probably did not exceed 5,000 or 7,000 worldwide. Rather than runaways, prostitutes, or drug addicts, most "models" were between the ages of seven and fourteen, came from middle-class homes, and knew the adults for whom they posed. Instances of infants being molested and photographed simultaneously are rare.

Combined, the United States and Europe from the late 1960s onward published fewer than 550 commercial child pornography magazines depicting children having sex with other children or adults, 460 magazines depicting boys nude, and fewer than 100 magazines depicting girls nude.[5] Some periodicals publicized as child pornography contained no sex or "lascivious exhibition of the genitals." *Moppets* was one of the better-known titles which does not qualify as child pornography despite testimony before Congress by such mendacious sources as Lloyd Martin of the Los Angeles Police Department.

Claims of child auctions in Amsterdam, toll-free numbers for ordering child prostitutes, and child "snuff" films are repeated endlessly by antiporn activists, but evidence has yet to be provided.

Robin Lloyd, author of the book *For Money or Love: Boy Prostitution in America*, claimed in the 1970s that there were 300,000 boys, aged eight to sixteen, in the pornography and prostitution rackets.[6] Dr. Judianne Densen-Gerber, whose efforts helped persuade Congress in 1977 to pass the first Sexual Exploitation of Minors Act, noted that Lloyd spoke only of boys. That led her to believe "that if there are 300,000 boys, there must be a like number of girls, but no one has bothered to count them. Lloyd postulated but cannot substantiate that only half the true number of these children is known. That would put the figure closer to 1,200,000 nationwide."[7]

Soon after child porn appeared on the shelves of sex shops around the country in the mid-1970s, moral crusaders stormed the country to decry the shameful exploitation of children by pornographers. "Articles and editorials appeared in nearly every newspaper in the United States calling for a stop to child pornography," wrote law professor Lawrence A. Stanley in a 1989 edition of the *Cardoza Arts and Entertainment Law Review*. "Within a year or two, in the face of mounting public pressure, distributors and retailers of adult pornography had removed child pornography from their stocks."[8]

Commercial child pornography ended in Denmark in 1980 when it became illegal. The last child pornography magazines out of Holland appeared in 1982.

> Despite this, the child pornography issue continued to be exploited nationwide [in the United States] by law enforcement officials, moral crusaders and the media. What may have begun as a legitimate concern for the well being of children quickly turned into a "moral panic" which swept the nation. Currently, child pornography slide shows and "teach-ins" continue to be given by law enforcement personnel, religious groups, Women Against Pornography, and other groups professing the danger that child pornography poses to children and society. Thousands of news articles, exposes, editorials, books, and television programs still proliferate at an astonishing rate, warning parents and children about kidnapping or sexual advances from strangers, neighbors, and, occasionally, relatives.[9]

The FBI's foremost expert on porn, Bill Kelly (who headed the MIPORN investigation), told the Meese Commission that "Kiddie porn has never been more than 1 percent of the total problem. But it gets 99 percent of the grease."[10]

In 1977, the Illinois House of Representatives appointed the Illinois Legislative Investigating Commission (ILIC) to look into child pornography.

> There is no evidence . . . that 300,000 or more children have ever been involved in these exploitative activities; that very few parents ever have offered their children to pornographers as

models . . . that there never was a nation-wide movement of children for sexual purposes. . . . [Sgt. Lloyd] Martin [of the LAPD] admitted that he had no firm statistics upon which to base his estimate and that, further, such statistics simply do not exist. . . . Our investigator then spoke with Robin Lloyd. . . . He stated that he had "thrown out" a figure of 300,000 as an estimate to see how law enforcement officials would react. . . . Though Lloyd's book contains numerous factual references, he appends neither footnotes nor bibliography; thus, it is impossible to check the veracity of anything he says.[11]

America's fight against a nonexistent child porn industry grew exponentially during the 1980s. United States Customs, the United States Postal Inspection Service, the Federal Bureau of Investigation, and state and local law enforcement and social service agencies established special units to combat the trade, which virtually ceased in 1978.

Two people largely caused the explosion of the kiddie porn myth into national hysteria: Sgt. Lloyd Martin and Judianne Densen-Gerber, the founder of the multinational drug rehabilitation organization Odyssey House. Martin told Congress that child porn was "worse than homicide."[12] Barbara Pruitt, an investigator for the LAPD, claimed that "the children who die, they are the lucky ones."[13] Densen-Gerber mailed child pornography to members of Congress and toured the country with stories of forced prostitution, drug addiction, kidnapping, and murder. She made numerous unsubstantiated claims, such as one in 1979 that "by recent count . . . there were 264 child pornography magazines being produced monthly and sold in adult bookstores across the country."[14]

Both Martin's and Densen-Gerber's crusading ended in 1982, but others swiftly replaced them. Kee MacFarlane, a social worker with Children's Institute International (CII) in

California, made the following statement to Congress in 1984 without providing any evidence to support her theories:

> I believe we're dealing with an organized operation of child predators designed to prevent detection. . . . The preschool, in such a case, serves as a ruse for a larger, unthinkable network of crimes against children. If such an operation involves child pornography or the selling of children, as is frequently alleged, it may have greater financial, legal and community resources at its disposal than those attempting to expose it.[15]

As with the hysteria over heterosexual transmission of the AIDS virus, the media did not let a lack of facts get in the way of a juicy story about kiddie porn. In its April 1983 issue, the *Ladies' Home Journal* reported that child pornography generates between $500 million and $1 billion annually, exploiting several million children. The *Albany Times Union* claimed that child pornography is a "$46 billion national industry—a loose network involving 2.4 million youngsters, according to federal statistics."[16] In 1988, Senator Dennis De Concini told Congress that "child pornography has become a highly organized multimillion-dollar industry."[17] These sources offered no evidence to back up their sensational claims.

The biggest domestic trafficker in child pornography is the federal government, whose sting operations encourage suspects to place ads seeking child porn. These fraudulent publications are the only ones in the United States today that solicit, advertise, sell, or offer to purchase or exchange child porn. Government agents also operate film laboratories which claim to provide confidential developing services. The Postal Inspection Service and Customs solicit tens of thousands to buy child porn videos, magazines, and photos from them. These forms of entrapment result in few arrests.

A person seeking child sex through magazines will only

find a vast network of postal inspectors and police. There are no sexually oriented publications in the United States today that contain ads for child porn. There are no toll-free numbers to order child prostitutes. There is no child porn industry. Or, at least, until the 1990s and the rise of the Internet, there wasn't.

◆◆◆◆

Because most of the world's religions and moral codes regard human-animal sex as loathsome, many countries prohibit bestiality. Few persons, however, are arrested for this crime. Scandinavia, which permits such sex, produces the best quality bestiality pix. During the 1970s, many sex shops offered explicit pictures of humans with dogs, pigs, donkeys, sheep, chicken, fish, and bulls. Finding models for such shoots is not easy. Though many porn girls do have sex with dogs, few, aside from American porn star Chessie Moore, permit photos of their escapades. (And Moore's film, which is untitled, is only available through private sales.) Under the direction of a Japanese film director "Tajirin," Bodil Joensen of Denmark starred in numerous bestiality films in the late 1960s and early 1970s. Hounded by the popular press, she committed suicide.

During the 1970s and 1980s, Reuben Sturman's Las Vegas partner Ralph Levine sold child porn and bestiality flicks through direct mail.[18] That he continued to sell kiddie porn beyond the 1970s is a novelty—as has been mentioned, the trade in such subjects had virtually ceased by 1978. And into the 1990s, pictures of bestiality could be bought from sex shops in San Francisco and New York. Today, bestiality is primarily viewed on the Internet, and much of that material is comprised of images scanned from 1970s' Scandinavian magazines.

Pornographers have long lived by the slogan "make love, not war." Explicit violence in porn is rarer than explicit plots. Most of the porn films that drip blood were made during the Golden Age. Anthony Spinelli directed 1975's *Defiance*—"a sexually more frightening film (and much more explicit) than *Straw Dogs*, or *The Snake Pit*, or even *Behind the Green Door*," writes critic Bob Rimmer. "Caught sniffing dope by her religious mother, [protagonist] Kathy is first sent to the psychiatric ward of a hospital where she is raped by the inmates and an attendant in a most brutally believable rape scene. 'Rescued' by a doctor who is a follower of the Marquis de Sade, she is tortured until horrifyingly, in the *Journey of O* tradition, she begins to enjoy her pain, debasement and degradation."[19]

David Fleetwood's *A Dirty Western* appeared in 1975. In the film, three convicts escape after seven years in prison. Jim, a rancher near the prison, leaves for a cattle drive while his wife, Sarah, plans her daughter's wedding. Jim and Sarah's goodbye, a gentle love scene, sets the prelude for the horror to come.

The three convicts come upon the ranch, and with Jim away, they rape Sarah and her daughters. "The film raises an inevitable question," writes Rimmer. "Why do violence, murder and rape make more sexually exciting films than stories dealing with normal emotions?"[20]

Porn historian Jim Holliday recommends *Story of Joanna* (1975) "as the best film example for a walk on the dark side of porn . . . an absolute must for those frustrated fetish freaks who are never satisfied in their search for kinky sadomasochism or bondage and discipline."[21]

Sadomasochistic porn particularly provokes industry critics. No civilization can be indifferent to the ways its citizens publicly entertain themselves, warns economist Walter Berns. "Bearbaiting and cockfighting are prohibited only in part out of compassion for the suffering animals. The main reason they were abolished was because it was felt that they debased and brutalized the citizenry who flocked to witness such spectacles."[22] Porn brutalizes and debases similarly, argues Irving Kristol, the father of neoconservatism. "We are not dealing with one passing incident—one book or one play or one movie. We are dealing with a general tendency that is suffusing our entire culture. Pornography differs from erotic art in that its whole purpose it to treat human beings obscenely, to deprive human beings of their specifically human dimension."[23]

"No one can prove that films with graphic sex or violence have a harmful effect on viewers," says commentator Arthur Lennig, "but there seems to be little doubt that films do have some effect on society and that all of us live with such effects. . . . The question of how society will function when all checks that a few thousand years of civilization have imposed have disappeared . . . has yet to be answered."[24]

Notes

1. "An Interview with Howard Ziehm," *Screw* (September 30, 1974).

2. Quoted by Bob Armstrong, "Snuff Films—Myth or Reality?" *Exotica* (February 1997): 53.

3. Quoted in ibid.

4. Quoted in ibid.

5. John Heidenry, *What Wild Ecstasy* (New York: Simon & Schuster, 1997), pp. 323–25; Lawrence A. Stanley, "The Child Porn Myth," *Cardoza Arts and Entertainment Law Review* (1989): 295–330.

6. Stanley, "The Child Porn Myth."

7. Ibid.

8. Ibid.

9. Ibid.

10. Ibid.

11. Ibid.

12. Ibid.

13. Ibid.

14. Ibid.

15. Ibid.

16. Cited in ibid.

17. Ibid.

18. Heidenry, *What Wild Ecstasy*, p. 214.

19. Robert Rimmer, *The X-Rated Videotape Guide* (Amherst, N.Y.: Prometheus Books, 1993), p. 77.

20. Ibid., p. 79.

21. Jim Holliday, *Only the Best* (Van Nuys, Calif.: Cal Vista Direct, Ltd., 1986), p. 77.

22. Quoted in Irving Kristol, *Reflections of a Neoconservative* (New York: Basic Books, 1983), p. 45.

23. Ibid.

24. Quoted in Rimmer, *The X-Rated Videotape Guide*, p. 34.

7.

Porn Stars

*R*unning the gamut from vicious to gentle, porn films of the 1970s—the Golden Age—used scripts, rehearsals, and other professional cinematic techniques. By the end of the decade it appeared that Hollywood and X might interpenetrate. Mainstream producers considered integrating real sex scenes into their movies while pornographers put real plots into theirs. This marriage between hardcore and pop culture was never consummated, however. Though mores changed drastically during the 1960s and 1970s, Americans remained stubbornly resistant to porn as just another product. Irresponsible with their brief years of freedom, pornographers soon found themselves on the defensive.

Numerous filmmakers like Chuck Vincent worked both sides of the fence. In *Roommates* and *In Love*, Vincent told real stories about real people, introducing porn to people who would never otherwise watch it and sparking cable TV's softcore explosion. Reality, however, is rarely sexy.

Vincent's most acclaimed film, *Roommates*, an X-rated attempt to cross over to the mainstream, appeared in 1981. Though celebrated by critics, it depressed the typical porn viewer who simply wanted to get off. "A couple of lesbian friends took it home," remembers porn star Veronica Hart, "and they said that the last thing they wanted to do afterward was to have sex."[1]

Considered the most artistic of all porn films, *In Love* appeared in 1983. A better sex film than *Roommates*, *In Love* chronicles a chance meeting between Kelly Nichols and Jerry Butler in a Florida bar. Following a passionate weekend, Butler returns to New York and Nichols heads for California. Twenty years pass before they meet again. Critics had quite a bit to say about the movie, but none of it was wholly positive: "*In Love* is the most successful failure of recent years," wrote Kent Smith for *Adam* magazine. "This is the X-rated industry's first . . . attempt at telling a swelling romantic love story. Both Jerry Butler and Kelly Nichols perform wonderfully. But the film never makes up its mind whether it's a grand erotic film or a badly made romance."[2] "If you're a newcomer [to pornography]," advises Steve Brent, "don't rent this film first. Save it for after you've seen some of the modern examples so you can appreciate what might have been if the forces of censorship and repression had never won their community-standards platform and banished sexuality from mainstream filmmaking."[3]

Overall, Vincent's movies fail as both porn and film. Other attempts include *Bon Appetit*, *Fascination*, *Puss 'n Boots*, *Bordello*, *Voyeur*, *Sex Drive*, and *Sex Crimes 2084*. Through these noble failures, Vincent helped turn porn in the opposite direction of his approach: Rather than more story and character development, X-rated movies since Vincent have concentrated on sex.

❖❖❖❖

Many consider Richard Mahler porn's greatest filmmaker even though his product, like Vincent's, was rarely erotic. *Her Name Was Lisa*, Mahler's most conventional film, appeared in 1979. In it massage girl Samantha Fox becomes a star model who slips into a bizarre world of kink. Offbeat and fixated with the morbid aspects of sex, Mahler leads the viewer into a world of strange characters. In his three decadent films that follow *Lisa*, which are set in the grimy streets of New York, Mahler does porn versions of Richard Wagner's opera trilogy, *The Ring*.

The Pink Ladies appeared in 1980. "Can anyone produce an adult film with almost continuous sex and almost no story line but so outrageous and far out that most men and women who watch it can't help laughing—or even occasionally identifying with the characters?" asks Bob Rimmer. "Richard Mahler has in this one."[4]

In 1982's *Midnight Heat*, Jamie Gillis plays a contract killer on the run after getting caught in bed with the wife of a mobster. More art than sex film, the encounters seem anti-erotic.

Gillis appears again in Mahler's third porno, playing a watcher in 1984's *Corruption*. In the film Bobby Astyr runs a decrepit bar with underground rooms where Gillis watches people indulge in promiscuous sex. The late Dan Stocket, one of the best porn reviewers, called *Corruption* the most splendid porn failure ever made because of its lack of eroticism.

The best films of Mahler and Vincent demonstrate how porn, at its most profound, rather than celebrating life, pisses on it. Few, if any, thinking pornographers settle for depicting hedonism. To directors like Mahler, Spinelli, and Damiano, the simple pursuit of pleasure is dull. Thus, you won't find a porn equivalent of *It's a Wonderful Life*. Fun porn, like *Deep Throat* and *Debbie Does Dallas*, is usually shallow. Deep porn (the original *Devil in Miss Jones*) is usually depressing, like the lives of many of the people in the industry.

Directing movies that ranged from the hilarious to the depressing, Ron Sullivan shot more pornos on film during the 1980s than anyone. "Most people think the average pornographer is a cigar-chomping, fat, middle-aged guy named Morty or Guido," writes *Genesis* magazine in its June 1980 issue. "So I would like to introduce them to New York-based producer-writer-director-distributor Ron Sullivan. In his late 30s, sporting fashionably long well-coifed hair and stylish glasses, Ron Sullivan's trademark is the three-piece suit."

An Irish-Protestant product of Middle America, Sullivan attended the University of Kansas City until it threw him out for excessive gambling. Drifting to New York City, he ended up in the film business, and between 1967 and 1980 produced fifteen films. In 1979, he directed his first porno— *Babylon Pink*. According to the June 1980 *Genesis*, Sullivan first wrote scripts under his own name. "I'd try to sell my pictures to buyers by telling them how great the movies were. And they'd say, 'What else would you say? You made the picture.' So I had to come up with a pseudonym. I chose Henri Pachard—initials H.P., which stand for 'High Profits.' "

"I was always into film—and when I saw the economics, I got into pornography. I acquired some pictures for another distributor and started to distribute without knowing how."

Porn before Sullivan resembled soap operas with sex thrown in. Sullivan focused the story of sex movies on sex and created dark and dirty dialogue that flowed from the characters making love. On the defensive during the Reagan years, pornographers like Sullivan created less controversial, more mainstream product with real plots, dialogue, and acting. Many tried to convince themselves that they no longer made porn, but "erotica."

In a May 1996 interview, Sullivan explained it this way:

> There are many people in this business who aren't sure why they're doing it and don't want to be doing it. It takes them a long time to get on the set. For various reasons they find little ways not to be there, and they find ways to get off the set. If I say cut, they'll get up and run and get a cigarette, so I tend not to cut, just keep the cameras rolling because there's part of them that's saying, "I shouldn't be doing this, I don't want to be doing this, I don't like doing this."[5]

Despite veiled attempts to convince themselves otherwise, participants in the porn industry were not merely creating erotica, and, ultimately, this is a large reason as to why they were successful. "Porn films are designed to be explicitly stimulating," veteran porn director Warren Evans explained to *Puritan* magazine. "Any eroticism is peripheral, around an explicit scene. . . . The guy who comes in needs that explicit stimulation, the graphic close-up, because he doesn't have it in his imagination."[6]

When pornographers try to move beyond formula, they begin to leave the masturbation genre. Explicit sex stymies such essential cinematic elements as plot development. Despite such limitations, directors like Sullivan tried to expand porn beyond its vulgar nature, using standard elements of filming to express more than simply the fulfillment of lust. One of the traditional elements of the X-rated formula to be employed in this manner—and one which was constantly under attack in the early 1980s—was the cum shot. Pulling out and jerking off on the woman denied the orgasmic experience. "When I made *Babylon Pink*," says Sullivan, "I tried to justify every proof shot, so at least it was credible. There's a reason for pulling out. The first is a routine, boring sex scene between a married couple. She is accommodating him and says, 'Don't cum in me. I'm not wearing anything.' And Bobby Astyr pulls out, cums on her navel and she routinely cleans it up. With the wipe of a Kleenex, you've established an attitude between two characters."[7]

With the increasing popularity of the VCR in the 1980s, porn returned to its loopy past. The comparatively lush movies of the Golden Age produced by such men as Gerard Damiano, Anthony Spinelli, Ron Sullivan, Lasse Braun, Chuck Vincent, and Alex deRenzy proved to be the exception in porn history, not the rule. The artistic statements these men tried to make were usually lost on the average viewer, and their films often failed. All six directors struggled to adapt to video and rarely produced anything of similar cinematic quality to their film best.

Adult movies, when judged as movies for adults, fail on any cinematic scale. No pornographic movie, not even *Misty Beethoven* or *Realm of the Senses*, would rank among the top 10,000 movies ever made. Despite the best efforts of Vincent, Mahler, and Sullivan, "Adult entertainment" remains a euphemism for "jerk off."

❖❖❖❖

During the mid-1980s, in the midst of hype about the transmission of AIDS between heterosexuals, the Mitchell brothers decided to remake 1972's *Behind the Green Door* as a safe-sex film. The sequel appeared in 1986, starring Artie Mitchell's girlfriend Missy (Elisa Flores). Before porn, she served as an aide to conservative senator Orrin Hatch (R-Utah).[8] The movie received mainstream attention for its casting of the Republican porn star and its use of condoms.

Missy appeared in a *Playboy* layout and on talk shows around the nation promoting the movie and its safe-sex theme. Jim Mitchell bragged it would make other porn films "obsolete." "If those other porn producers didn't like it," he said, "tough shit. It's a whole new world out there."

Jim's pride went before a mighty fall. Despite the abundant publicity, *Behind the Green Door II* flopped. *Screw* called it the most disappointing sex flick of the year.[9] It had all the typical Mitchell Brothers problems—garbled sound, no plot, poor lighting, and amateurish camerawork.

In 1991, Jim Mitchell, frustrated by his brother's erratic ways, murdered Artie. He then hired a clever lawyer who bamboozled judge and jury into a "voluntary manslaughter" conviction carrying a maximum punishment of six years in prison. After serving three years, Jim was released in 1997.

❖❖❖❖

One of history's three leading female performers, along with Marilyn Chambers and Ginger Lynn, was Seka (a Serbo-Croatian term of endearment for a little girl), who debuted in porn at the peak of the Golden Age.

Born in 1954, Seka grew up in Radford, Virginia. She graduated from beauty pageants to modeling, appearing in such magazines as *Vanity Fair*, *Interview*, and *Metro*. At the suggestion of Ken Yontz, the owner of several sex shops, Seka answered an ad in a Los Angeles paper for nude models and made her first sex film, a fifteen-minute, 8mm loop shot by porn director Scotty Fox. She was twenty-two. It was the first time she'd been outside Virginia.[10]

Seka became a video queen, appearing in such early releases as *Seka's Fantasies*, produced by the Caballero film company. *Playboy* called her "a bona fide video phenomenon—just like Boy George and stereo television."[11] A decade after *Deep Throat* launched the age of porno chic, Seka's publicity machine heralded her as the star who'd inherit the sex-goddess mantle of Marilyn Monroe and bridge the gap between hardcore and mainstream. *Chicago Tribune* journalist Eric Zorn interviewed Seka about her dreams in November 1982. She lived at the time with her manager who promoted her as "The Total Woman of the '80s."

"America is ready for quality porn," Seka's manager told Zorn. "Seka will bring sex out of the closet and into the homes of everyone."[12] Seka claimed her autobiography was in the works at a major New York publishing house and she'd received several offers from mainstream movie producers.

"It seemed to make sense back then," recalls Zorn. "The home video revolution had just started to take off and explicit sex tapes for home viewing were a novelty and a rage. . . . Many in the porn industry believed this entrée to the family rooms of middle America heralded the mainstreaming of their tawdry art. High-concept hard-core and family comedies would someday run side by side at the Cinema 10. Catch the wave, right?"[13]

An editor whose wisdom Zorn will only now acknowledge thought the whole idea so unlikely that he spiked the story. Seka's autobiography never appeared. Her mainstream work amounted to a background role as a porn star in *Men Don't Leave*. She split from and successfully sued her manager for stealing from her.

Twenty pounds overweight, Seka returned to porn in Ron Sullivan's 1993 film *American Garter*, "the biggest disappointment since Traci Lords's videos were pulled off the shelves," says the *Hustler Erotic Video Guide* (*HEVG*). "Seka is an older broad now, but older chicks can still fuck with enthusiasm (Nina Hartley for example). Seka has lost her sexual appeal and now looks like that middle-aged aunt of yours whose support hose bunches at the knees."[14]

Porn acting reached its peak in the early 1980s thanks to the efforts of thespians like Veronica Hart, perhaps the best porn actress ever. Sam Frank dedicated his book *Sex in Cinema* to her in hopes that she'd achieve mainstream success. She hasn't.

Hart's life changed at age twenty when she accidentally spilled scalding coffee on her side. She spent two months in the hospital.

> You don't have to be a psychology expert to see why I got into porn. I've always liked sex but my life would probably have taken a different turn without that accident.
>
> People in pornography are usually rebels or are trying to make up for some kind of deficiency or defect. It could be in their character or they could've been beaten or sexually abused in their childhood or their nose is crooked or some other physical defect.
>
> At one point in the hospital, I felt that I'd never be able to take off my clothes in front of a man. On the first night I spent with my English boyfriend after getting out of hospital, he turned off the lights. And I like to make love with the lights on. So that hurt.[15]

With a bachelor of arts in theater and a background in modeling and straight films, Hart moved to New York, where she worked as a temporary secretary. Roy Stewart, who had done X-rated films, saw Hart's modeling pictures and acting credits. He told her she was wasting her time, "selling [her] brains, . . . time, . . . organizational ability, everything, for not much money."[16] So Hart entered the world of performance sex, first performing in front of theater audiences on Broadway, although she also enjoyed sex in front of the camera. Like several of the directors previously discussed, Hart would like to see more character development in porn. "Have the story tell how the couple gets to fucking. A lot of bad porn has fucking every other scene, and that's not how it is in real life. . . . A good porn movie is one you could take all the sex scenes out and still have a good movie."[17]

Of course, not everyone agrees with this point. By contrast, Al Goldstein, publisher of *Screw* magazine, says, "The plot of a porn film is like the frame of a painting. You don't look at the frame."[18]

Despite this common sentiment, Hart sees porn as a business in transition. "People are trying to do different things, and make it more realistic," she says. "The women's market is untapped. There are films [I starred in] that I dearly love [*Amanda by Night*, *Scent of Heather*, and *Roommates*]. They've been criticized and aren't played in theaters because they don't have all the open cum-shots. They're not considered explicit enough."[19]

"*Amanda by Night* was like a TV movie with sex in it," Hart told me during a 1996 interview. "You look at it as before he [director Robert McCallum] was comfortable doing sex and I look at it as when he was a real filmmaker."[20] In *Amanda*, Hart plays a hooker who breaks free of her pimp and cares about her clients. Despite this cliché of the hooker with a heart of gold, the film's mixture of sex and violence keeps the viewer's interest to the romantic ending.

Hart quit doing explicit sex scenes after four years in the biz, but she still makes cameo appearances in porn. Although she played a judge in the 1997 R-rated film *Boogie Nights*, overall, however, the mainstream film industry has not been as warm and inviting as Hart's on-screen vagina. She's mustered only small roles in big movies and only big roles in small movies.

Like numerous other stars, Hart left performing in porn

to marry and have children. At VCA, one of the largest porn producers, she makes porn videos under her real name, Jane Hamilton, and directs as Veronica Hart. "I make pornography because I can . . . and because mainstream isn't beating down my door."[21]

> A writer from one of those classy women's magazines wanted to know what changes women had made in the business. And I said "None." Maybe there's a genre that hasn't been developed yet. There are two women making sex videos for women. We've been neglected. You've either got the slut who loves fuck films like the guys or the woman who never wants one of those films in the home. Most women are in between. They do enjoy sex but they need to be courted . . . with production value and romance. And there are also guys like that. I believe there's a whole niche for sex stores like Victoria's Secret with vibrators and selected videos. . . .
>
> It's always been an easy thing to say—"I've done porn films, they won't let me cross over." There are a lot of things that won't let you cross over. If you hadn't done porn, you'd still have no chance to make it.[22]

Hart appeared in many movies with her friend Kelly Nichols, one of porn's best actresses. Growing up in a small suburb of Los Angeles with four older brothers, Nichols was a tomboy. Leaving home at age eighteen, the brunette moved to Hollywood where she opened a copy of *Free Press* and read an ad for Sunset International. "Reb Sawitz got me my first real professional modeling jobs. Boy, some of the doozies they threw at you. Little girl from the suburbs and you have photographers chasing you around the house. Craziness. But it was good training."[23]

Nichols moved to New York in 1979, where her husband introduced her to Chuck Vincent, who was looking for the female and male leads in *Bon Appetit*. Vincent offered Nichols $12,000 and two weeks in Europe. She needed the money as well as the opportunity to rebuild her self-confidence.

Vincent shot the two weeks in Europe, waited a month, shot a week of straight scenes in New York, and then crammed all the sex scenes into one week. When confronted with a week of back-to-back sex, Nichols approached it like a football game. "I go from here to here, and at the end I get the rest of the money."[24]

Nichols felt troubled by the attention she earned spreading her legs.

> I didn't know I had a pretty face and I hated my body. So how did I think I was a porn star, making my body naked and putting on makeup and being called beautiful?
>
>   I'd go to shoots and drink because I needed to feel calm. I think 25 was a watermark year, because you're a quarter of a century old, and you think, "What do I do when I grow up? In five years I'll be 30, and people aren't going to tolerate this."[25]

Nichols did three mainstream films in the summer of 1983, finding that producers in New York did not care about her porn background. She appeared in *Model Behavior*, *Unknown*, and *C.H.U.D.—Cannibalistic Humanoid Underground Dwellers*. A few years later, Nichols was Jessica Lange's stunt double in the remake of *King Kong*.

After retiring from hardcore, Nichols settled down with her boyfriend and had two children. She eventually followed her boyfriend to Los Angeles when his screenwriting career took off with such hits as *Nightmare on Elm Street 4*. She now goes by the name Marianne Walter and does make-up for X-rated and mainstream productions.

❖❖❖❖

Before she was replaced by Kelly Nichols and Veronica Hart, mercurial Samantha Fox aka Stasia Micula was Chuck Vincent's favorite star. Despite quality performances in over one hundred features, Micula never made it to the X-Rated Critics Organization's Hall of Fame because of her criticism of the industry.

Micula studied art at Sarah Lawrence College in Westchester County, New York. She began modeling nude, which led to prostitution and eventually porn. "My husband suggested that I get into nude pictures. About three months later, I walked into this office and the guy said, 'I want to use you for the lead in my movie.' " Stasia asked her husband if she could do the porno and he asked her how much money she'd make. Micula said she hoped to make lots of money. He told her to go for it.[26]

Micula entered porn in 1977. Her favorite film was her first—*Here Cums the Bride*—but *Her Name Was Lisa* most closely resembled her life. "At the time I was a drug addict. I had to play an addict that goes from bad to worse. It happens to a lot of hookers. I liked it because the acting was juicy. I got to die, lie in a coffin for six hours.[27]

In the early 1990s, Micula was working toward a degree in physical therapy from Hunter College while making her living by teaching aerobics to elderly ladies in posh Fifth Avenue apartments.

❖❖❖❖

Jerry Butler, who's given name is Paul Seiderman, was porn's best actor. His autobiography, *Raw Talent* (1990), goes beyond criticizing the porn industry and its leading personalities. Many of its stories are exaggerated if not fabricated and the book effectively ended Butler's tenure in the biz. He says that the only people he knows in porn who still like him are pornographer William Margold and his friends about whom he didn't write.

Butler says he's been a sex freak since age three, when he began masturbating. At age seven he watched porno films on his dad's 8mm projector. At thirteen, Butler lost his virginity to a prostitute. At eighteen, while studying acting in New York, Butler found himself surrounded by gays wanting to seduce him.[28]

Scanning through *Backstage*, Butler came across an ad looking for extras on a porno set. He answered the call and did his first flick, 1979's *Wet, Wild and Wonderful*, directed by Jim Clark. "In my first scene, a woman gave me head. She sucked my cock in an unbelievable way and I came all over her face. I discovered she was a drug addict. Maybe my cock represented her next fix and that was why she sucked it with such desperation."[29]

After three days' work, Butler walked away with several hundred dollars. He promised himself that he'd never again do porn, a determination he repeated over the next dozen years. But "Jerry Butler" kept doing porn until porn no longer wanted him.

Butler appeared in Chuck Vincent's *Roommates*, which opened at New York's 8th Street Playhouse, a theater that usually runs general-release movies. Critic Judith Crist gave the movie a good review and singled out Butler's performance. Generally, however, the film did not do well. "People in the business didn't take *Roommates* seriously," writes Butler in his autobiography. "Somebody looking to get off would rather see five barrels of cum on some girl's face than emotion and drama."[30] Butler, like many of his peers, did not want to make porn.

Porn's biggest male star, John Holmes, died of an AIDS-related illness March 13, 1988.[31] Holmes had sex with thousands of women on- and off-screen, and also with men, though he didn't boast about that. "John considered it as satisfying to stick his dick into a guy as into a pussy," says Jim Holliday.[32]

Holmes did two generations of porn stars—from Seka and Marilyn Chambers to Ginger Lynn and the Italian member of Parliament Ilona "Ciccolina" Staller. He appeared in about 2,500 flicks including gay ones.

Holmes's private life also revolved around his penis. Rich men and women paid handsomely to play with it, and although porn has seen longer dicks (Dick Rambone measured fifteen inches), none is as famous.

Bob Chinn produced and directed Holmes's most successful series, *Johnny Wadd*, where he played a hard-boiled detective. "Holmes was everyman's gigolo," writes *Rolling Stone* (June 15, 1989), "a polyester smoothy with a sparse moustache, a flying collar and lots of buttons undone. He took a lounge singer's approach to sex, deliberately gentle, ostentatiously artful, a homely guy with a pinkie ring and a big dick who was convinced he was every woman's dream."

Born on August 8, 1944, in Pickaway County, Ohio, John Curtis Holmes was the youngest of four children. His mother, a Bible-thumping Baptist, spent much of her marriage yelling at her husband, a carpenter and alcoholic who'd throw up on the kids. Holmes lost his virginity at age twelve to a thirty-six-year-old friend of his mother. After serving in the army, Holmes began driving an ambulance at age nineteen. He met a nurse, Sharon Gebenini, who worked at USC County General on a team pioneering open-heart surgery. In August 1965, they married.

One afternoon three years later, Sharon came home early from work to find John measuring his penis. She went into her bedroom and lay down. Twenty minutes later John appeared. He had a full erection.

"It's incredible," said John.

"What?"

"It goes from five inches all the way to ten. Ten inches long! Four inches around!"

"That's great," said Sharon, turning a page of her magazine. "You want me to call the press?"

John stared at her for a long time before he spoke. "I've got to tell you that I've been doing something else, and I think I want to make it my life's work."[33]

That encounter marked the beginning of the end of their relationship, though it stumbled on for another twelve years.

While on disability because of a collapsed lung received while driving a forklift, Holmes had answered an ad for porn performers placed by William Amerson, who became the porn star's close friend and manager over the next twenty years. He was one of the few people to whom Holmes told as much truth as lies.

Holmes quickly earned lots of money. He became a star. In 1978, at the height of his career, Holmes earned $3,000 a day from porn and almost as much selling himself as a gigolo. But, according to a June 15, 1989, article published in *Rolling Stone*, he had a drug problem spinning out of control. Every ten to fifteen minutes he needed a hit of coke and then forty to fifty Valium a day to cut the edge.

As his drug use increased, Holmes became harder to work with. People on the set joked that you had to leave a trail of freebase from the bathroom to the bedroom to get him to work.

Drugs eventually killed Holmes's abilities to get hard on camera. The man who claimed to earn half-a-million dollars a year from his sexual talents in 1980 became a drug delivery boy for a gang of outlaws and junkies.[34]

In 1976, Holmes had begun courting fifteen-year-old

Dawn Schiller. He bought her stuffed animals, roses, and a ring. One night, John drove Dawn to the beach in his van and stole her heart and virginity. John got Dawn hooked on drugs and eventually had her turning tricks to support his drug habit. John and Dawn lived for months out of Sharon's Chevy Malibu. Eventually, Holmes got his girlfriend into an apartment in the San Fernando Valley with a porn actress and high-priced hooker named Michelle. Dawn continued to turn tricks to support Holmes's drug habit. Committing felony crimes most days, Holmes stole luggage off conveyors at Los Angeles International Airport and bought appliances with his wife's credit cards and traded them for cash. Police finally caught him January 14, 1981, stealing a computer out of a car.[35]

Nightclub owner and drug kingpin Adel "Eddie Nash" Nasrallah bailed John and Dawn out of jail (Dawn had been arrested as an accessory to the crime). Holmes had met Nash several years earlier. The Palestinian loved porn and loved John, treating him beautifully. Holmes thought Nash the most evil man he'd ever met but he couldn't figure him out. So Holmes just hung around, even presenting Dawn to Nash on his birthday in 1980. Nash was so pleased he gave John a quarter pound of hard cocaine.[36]

After their release from jail, Dawn fled. John chased her to the bus station but Dawn had convinced the clerk there to give Holmes the wrong information by saying her life was at stake. Holmes followed the wrong bus all the way to San Francisco. He then returned to Sharon and beat her up. Dawn got home to Oregon and for months refused to answer John's phone calls. Eventually she relented.[37]

Five months after fleeing him, Dawn reunited with Holmes in West Los Angeles two days before the most frightening week of Holmes's life.

In late June 1981, Holmes was in bad shape. He'd smoked a couple of drug deliveries for the Wonderland Gang, a group of drug dealers who lived in a stucco house on Wonderland Avenue, a steep, winding road in the hills above Hollywood. Holmes owed them and Eddie Nash money.

The Wonderland gang was out of drugs, out of money, and out of patience with Holmes. They demanded that he take them to Nash.

Holmes did and the gang made Nash plead for his life before stealing over $100,000 cash, jewelry, and more than eight pounds of cocaine from him. After going back to their place on Wonderland Avenue, the gang divided up the spoils. John Holmes got several thousand dollars, cocaine, and jewelry.[38]

While wearing a ring stolen in the robbery, Holmes was caught in the San Fernando Valley by Nash's three-hundred-pound karate-expert bodyguard Gregory DeWitt Niles, a convicted felon. Niles dragged Holmes to the furious Nash. The druglord threatened Holmes that he'd murder Holmes's friends and family if he didn't lead them to the Wonderland gang. According to various reports, including *Rolling Stone* (June 15, 1989), *Playboy* (March 1998), and *Wadd*, a 1999 documentary produced by VCA films, Holmes took Nash and his associates to the house on Wonderland Avenue where the gang stayed. The entire gang was later found slain, although it is not clear whether they had already been murdered by other thugs when Holmes and company arrived, or if Nash and Niles and perhaps Holmes did the dirty deed.[39]

Early that Thursday morning, July 2, Holmes, covered with blood, knocked at Sharon's door. He told her he'd been in a car accident. Sharon, a nurse, bathed him. She didn't notice any abrasions. Sharon questioned Holmes because she could tell by the look in his eyes that he was lying. John then confessed to Sharon the truth of what happened.

"Why didn't you do something?" Sharon asked.

"I couldn't," said John. "It was either me and my family, including you, or them. They made Nash beg for his life. They deserved to die."[40]

John went to Dawn and fell asleep. She heard him cry out in his sleep, "Blood, blood, blood, so much blood." On the late TV news she saw the report on the murders of the four Wonderland gangsters. She put everything together and waited until morning. After Holmes awoke, he told Schiller a made-up story.

A week later, police took John, Dawn, and Sharon into custody, billeting them at a luxury hotel. Holmes enjoyed the attention and told the police everything except who killed the Wonderland gang. Holmes refused to testify because he feared that Nash would murder his family. After a few days, the police released the three. Dawn and Sharon dyed John's hair black. Dawn and John spray-painted Sharon's Chevy Malibu and then the two of them took off across the country. Holmes broke into cars along the way to finance their journey.

When they arrived in Miami, Holmes got Schiller turning tricks at the beach. When she tired of it, he publicly beat her, so she ran away. A couple weeks later, on December 4, 1981, Schiller led the police to Holmes. It was the last time that John and Dawn saw each other.

Holmes went on trial for murdering the Wonderland gang. Because of his fear of Eddie Nash, he refused to testify in his own defense. He used a simple defense: John Holmes was the "sixth victim" of the Wonderland murders, and Eddie Nash was "evil incarnate."

"Ladies and gentleman," said Holmes's lawyer at the beginning of the trial, "unlike some mysteries, this is not going to be a question of 'Who done it?' This is going to be a question of 'Why aren't the perpetrators here?'" The jury acquitted Holmes.[41]

Months earlier, the police had arrested Nash, his bodyguard Niles, and others on charges of drug possession and drug selling. On November 22, 1982, Nash received the maximum sentence of eight years in jail. Upon hearing the news, John Holmes testified that same day before a grand jury (testimony before a grand jury is not part of the public record) and was released.

Almost forty, Holmes returned to porn as the grand old man. In *California Valley Girls*, for instance, he has one scene. He enters the room and sits on a couch. A girl comes in and begins sucking him, followed by another girl, and then a third. Eventually, six girls work on his penis.

In early 1985, while working on *Fleshpond*, Holmes met Laurie Rose, who was nineteen. Her porn name was Misty Dawn. A junkie who came from a small town outside Vegas, she looked like Holmes's old girlfriend Dawn Schiller. Misty appeared in such flicks as *Aerobisex Girls #1*, *Desire*, and *Nasty Nurses*.

In 1986, Holmes tested HIV-positive. He smoked several packs of cigarettes a day in addition to ingesting enormous amounts of alcohol and drugs with Misty. Despite his disease, he kept doing porn, including *The Rise and Fall of the Roman Empress*, starring Ilona "Ciccolina" Staller, a future member of the Italian parliament.

Pain dominated the last two years of John's life. In late 1987, Holmes married Laurie Rose (Misty) at the Little Chapel of the Flower in Las Vegas. On March 13, 1988, he died. Six months later, on September 8, 1988, Nash and Niles were charged with the murders on Wonderland Avenue but were acquitted.

Notes

1. Personal interview with Veronica Hart, April 1996.
2. Kent Smith, "In Love," *Adam* (October 1983): 32.
3. Steve and Elizabeth Brent, *Couples Guide to the Best Erotic Videos* (New York: St. Martin's Press, 1997), pp. 103–104.
4. Robert Rimmer, *The X-Rated Videotape Guide* (Amherst, N.Y.: Prometheus Books, 1993), p. 117.
5. Personal interview with Ron Sullivan, May 1996.
6. "Porn Talk," *Puritan* no. 8 (1984).
7. Ibid.
8. Steve Chapple and David Talbot, *Burning Desires: Sex in America, a Report from the Field* (New York: Signet, 1990), p. 214.
9. John Hubner, *Bottom Feeders* (New York: Doubleday, 1992), p. 337.
10. Mary T. Schmich, "Star of Film Fantasies Satisfied Staying Dressed for Success," *Chicago Tribune*, October 11, 1985.
11. Ibid.
12. Eric Zorn, "Seka Can't Seem to Find Big Time," *Chicago Tribune*, November 17, 1992.
13. Ibid.
14. "American Garter," *Hustler Erotic Video Guide* (October 1993): 22.
15. Hart interview.
16. Ibid.
17. Ibid.
18. Ibid.
19. Ibid.
20. Ibid.
21. Ibid.
22. Ibid.
23. "Kelly Nichols," *Adam* (October 1993): 18.

24. Ibid.

25. Ibid.

26. "Here Cums Samatha Fox," *Swank* (June 1987): 43.

27. Ibid.

28. Jerry Butler, *Raw Talent* (Amherst, N.Y.: Prometheus Books, 1990), pp. 69–72.

29. Ibid., p. 75.

30. Ibid., p. 84.

31. Heidenry, *What Wild Ecstasy*, p. 240.

32. Personal interview with Jim Holliday, April 18, 1996.

33. Mike Sager, "The Devil and John Holmes," *Rolling Stone* (June 15, 1989): 53.

34. Ibid., p. 55.

35. Ibid.

36. Ibid. Other sources include *Wadd*, a 1999 documentary directed by Wesley Emerson and produced by VCA.

37. Ibid.

38. Ibid.

39. Ibid.

40. Ibid., p. 57.

41. Ibid.

8.

Fallen Angels

In 1983, Stanford University graduate Gregory Dark coproduced the documentary *Fallen Angels*, which profiles newcomers Kristarra Barrington, "Clarissa," and "Kim." "In my more naive days," says agent Jim South, "I allowed [a *Fallen Angels* coproducer] to shoot for three days at my office. She then proceeded to sell the footage to every dirtbag in the world. Her documentary portrays pornographers as persons who beat their wives and fuck their children."[1]

Fallen Angels gave South an early signal that Dark was trouble. Despite this warning sign, the two men continued their association, and in the 1980s, they ran a dance agency together. Unbeknownst to South, Dark turned the agency into an escort service. Dark eventually served nine months in prison for pimping and he has rarely spoken with South since.

Early in the documentary and early in their porn careers, Kim, Clarissa, and Kristarra visit director Bruce "Seven" Behan who tells them, much to their disgust, to stuff each other full of dildos. Afterward, the girls say they'll never work for him again. South appears shocked that Behan uses dildos and assures the girls that he'll have nothing further to do with the man.

A few months later, Behan moved next door to Dark and received a steady supply of fresh talent from the World Modeling office.

Fallen Angels covers the making of *Caught from Behind 2*, which later got busted by the police, leading to the California Supreme Court's important *Freeman* decision which effectively legalized porn in the state. *Fallen Angels'* three leading protagonists appear to be devastated by porn. Clarissa's biker boyfriend, David, resents having "his old lady poked on screen. I can't handle another guy touching my woman."[2]

Director Hal Freeman remembers a porn star whose boyfriend tried to kill her after watching her perform sex with another guy on camera. "Every guy who goes out with a performer is going to get angry. He'll say 'That's my property being used and abused.' "[3]

Kristarra Barrington lied to her boyfriend about doing boy-girl scenes. "I feel bad about lying. . . . But you get more money to do boy-girl and we need the money."[4]

Cut. Barrington's boyfriend says, "Kristarra doesn't like to have sex with strangers."[5]

Cut. Barrington: "I slept with 260 guys in high school."[6]

Five months into her career, Barrington says she doesn't want to do porn much longer. "You're just a piece of meat. You have no say. . . . You do what they say."[7]

Eighteen months later, after Kim's unexplained disappearance and Clarissa's retirement, Kristarra, still in her relationship with an unhappy boyfriend, remained in porn, ranking as one of the leading Asians of the 1980s.

Fallen Angels depicts talent agent Jim South as a shifty salesman. "I sold insurance and loved it," says South. "I find that the training I got selling people cold, even in this business, helps me a lot because you're selling the girls on modeling. You're trying to explain to girls that they can trust you."[8]

Perhaps the girls can trust Jim South. But can Jim South trust the girls? Later in 1993, South apparently got snowed by "Traci Lords."

In an article that appeared in the April 1990 *GQ*, journalist Pat Jordan provides a brief biography of Nora Louise Kuzma (Traci Lords). Born May 7, 1968, Lords moved to Redondo Beach in southern California with her mother and sisters in 1980, fleeing emotional abuse by her alcoholic father. She soon lost her virginity, got pregnant, and despite her boyfriend's offer of marriage, had an abortion. In 1983, at age fifteen, Kuzma ran away to Los Angeles. She lived with a man in his forties who posed as her stepdad when they visited Jim South's World Modeling agency. Kuzma showed South a California driver's license and a birth certificate bearing the name Kristie Nussbaum and the birth date November 17, 1963.

World Modeling first sent Lords to a shoot simulating sex, but the photographer had to stop filming because Lords took it past simulation.

Traci Lords made her video debut in 1984's *What Gets Me Hot*, earning $200 a day. A scared brunette who still had her baby fat, Lords kept glancing sideways at the camera during her early performances. Her hands shook.

"Traci Lords sat naked on the couch where that cat is now," veteran pornographer Bill Margold remembers.

> It was 1985 and my wife Drea and I were going to do a movie called *Portrait of Lust*. I said to Drea that there's something wrong with this girl. She sat there looking like a lump, a wet

looking, unformed lump. She wasn't formed properly. She had these conical tits, baby fat and the dullest look I have ever seen on a female. And I couldn't put together that this was an underage female. If I had caught her, think of the misery that I could've prevented. I keep reliving that day. Obviously, something stopped me from asking her if she was under eighteen. Maybe the hell-bent rush-to-disaster mentality of the industry, maybe its deathwish, exists within me as well.[9]

Within months of entering the industry, though, Lords transformed herself into a tough blonde who battled her male counterparts.

Porn customers around the world adored Lords. She got mobbed in Paris and Tokyo. At adult video conventions, male fans waited hours to get her autograph.

Earning over $1 million from porn, Lords raised her own financing, produced her own films, wrote her own scripts, starred in her own projects, and marketed the resulting product. She formed Traci Lords Productions with her "manager" and boyfriend, a man in his late thirties whom Jim South describes as a "snake."[10] According to journalist Pat Jordan, Lords and her boyfriend got video companies to pay Lords $10,000 a month and furnish her with an apartment and a Mercedes. Shortly after she turned eighteen, Lords raised somewhere between $25,000 to $50,000 from a video distributor to make a porno in Paris. Though she went to France, she told the distributor she never made the movie.

On a Saturday afternoon in May 1986, shortly after she returned to California, federal agents arrested Lords for being under the age of consent (eighteen) when she made seventy-seven X-rated flicks. Video stores pulled all her movies within hours of the news and porn distributors destroyed millions of dollars' worth of tapes.

Lords claims she can't remember her porn career because

of the large amounts of drugs she ingested. But she is sure that she made only a handful of films and that producers took clips from those few to display her in seventy-seven titles. Lords claims she made less than $50,000 in porn and spent most of it on drugs. In short, she claims she was a victim of drugs, unhappiness, and most of all, pornographers. "I never saw any of my movies," Lords told *GQ.* "I don't even remember making them. I was drinking and addicted to drugs."

Those who knew her laugh at this assertion. "Is that what she's claiming now?" asks Jim South. "That's an absolute lie. I never saw the girl take drugs. I would've had complaints. She was always a responsible businesswoman."[11]

Former Los Angeles County district attorney Ira Reiner said, "She may well be a hard professional now, but she was fifteen . . . when the pornographic film industry got a hold of her. The thrust of our investigation is directed toward the industry that exploited her."[12]

Lords was never charged with a crime, although several pornographers (including Jim South and pornographer Rubin Gottesman) spent a total of about $1 million to defend themselves from charges of sexually exploiting a minor. Federal law makes it illegal to hire someone underage for pornography, even if one doesn't know that they're underage. But California state court went easy, and Jim South got off without going to jail. Rubin Gottesman, however, received a one-year sentence for selling Traci Lords tapes after it became public knowledge that she'd lied about her age. Lords claims she spent thousands of dollars on legal fees but for what purpose is not clear, as she was never charged with anything.

Lords did make a porno in Paris just before returning to California and being arrested. While condemning porn and claiming "victim" status after her arrest, she sold *Traci I Love*

You to a distributor for $100,000. It's the only porno legally available in America featuring Lords, although her other films are easy to find in some video stores.

After disappearing from public sight for a few years, Lords returned in 1988 as a B-film bimbo and nudie poster girl. She says that during the silent years she got her life straightened out by joining Alcoholics Anonymous and Narcotics Anonymous. By 1989, Lords had a Hollywood agent—Don Geller—and she decided to quit doing nude scenes. She's lived up to her word, turning down numerous movie offers.

Traci the porn star slept with many of the industry's leading producers and directors but the new Traci told *GQ* she won't sleep with someone to get a part. "Just because I'm young and pretty doesn't mean I'm bait. I'm not for sale. I don't believe in fucking fat, stupid, Jewish producers to get a role."[13]

The complex, perky blonde sings on such albums as *Little Baby Nothing* by the Manic Street Preachers and *Somebody to Love* by the Ramones; acts in B-movies such as *Nowhere*, *Blood Money*, and *Skinner*, and turns up occasionally on TV programs such as *Melrose Place*.

"If you're sexy, everybody will love you," Lords said in 1995. "That's what I wanted—for everybody to love me."[14]

Whenever it has become public knowledge that a porn performer was underage, producers, distributors, and store-owners have pulled offending copies of his or her movies. In November 1991, distributors destroyed sixty titles featuring Canadian actress Alexandra Quinn, who was under eighteen when she performed in them. Using fake ID, the busty blonde began stripping in clubs at age fifteen to get attention and money from men. When she saw the lust and dollars directed toward porn star Erica Boyer on a strip appearance, Quinn decided that she, too, wanted to do porn. Boyer introduced Quinn to Jim South, who checked her identification. The ID was fake, however, as Quinn admitted to *Hustler Erotic Video Guide*: "I did a lot of cutting and pasting with my birth certificate, using the copy machine. I made my own ID. It wasn't good enough to get into bars but they let me do movies with it."[15]

Quinn flew from Canada to Los Angeles with just enough money to pay for a couple of meals. To support her cocaine habit, which she had picked up after just a few weeks in the industry, Quinn made about sixty videos before turning eighteen. One day on set she forgot her fake ID (IDs were checked for each production) so she used her real ID, figuring no one would notice. She was wrong. The discovery of her youthful status resulted in all of her films being withdrawn from circulation.[16]

Quinn condemned the industry on the TV show *Hard Copy* and was blackballed by many pornographers. "For a long time I was angry. All the people I thought were my friends turned their backs on me."[17] Needing money, Quinn returned to porn a couple of years later.

Traci Lords and Alexandra Quinn are just two porn stars who began performing before they were over the legal age to do so. Lydia Chanel, who started in France, admits she did fifteen pornos before turned eighteen. Other actresses guilty of the same crime include Tabatha Cash, Renee Summers, Kristarra Barrington, Ali Moore, Nikki Charm, and Christiana.

Many of the Traci Lords movies costarred video queen Ginger Lynn Allen. Born in 1962, Allen lives in southern California but strips at clubs across the nation. Born and raised in Rockford, Illinois, Allen says she left her hometown for the first time at age nineteen to visit her ailing grandfather in California. She decided to stay. She managed the Musicland store in Redlands, living in a tiny trailer in one of the worst parts of town. She led a normal life with a boring boyfriend and job. Wanting more, she answered an ad in September 1983 for "attractive female models for work paying $150 to $2,000 a day." That same day she received an offer to pose for *Penthouse*. Allen regarded such magazines, which her father had left around the house, as "neat." "They didn't seem wrong. I thought the girls were all pretty and that boys liked these kind of girls. I never imagined I could be one of them."[18]

As good as $150 a day was, after three months, Allen wanted more, so she jumped on a $1,000-a-day offer to make videos in Hawaii with Jerry Butler. Arriving at their motel in Hawaii, Ginger and Jerry launched into bouts of raunchy sex and deep conversation. She confessed her worries about "acting" to her more experienced costar. The rape scene in *A Little Bit of Hanky Panky* particularly scared her. The script called for Jerry to chase Ginger on a motorcycle. With Allen unable to muster the proper emotion, Butler played an acting trick on her.

According to Allen, the most important person in her life was her grandfather, who had recently died. So Jerry told Ginger that old people should be left to die. She became angry, and then Jerry gave her the script and said, "Do the scene that way."[19]

After having known each other only six days, Jerry and Ginger began to talk about moving in together. Butler left the islands early to work on *Taboo 3*. A few days later, he bought a small pre-engagement ring, wrapped it in a seven-foot box and then drove to the airport to pick Ginger up. She wasn't on the plane and that was the end of their romance.

Porn's last big star, Allen became famous for the "Ginger" video series written by Raven Touchstone. The original Vivid Girl (which can be equated to being a Playboy Bunny), Allen invested money in the new company (Vivid) in

1985 and helped its climb to the top. "It's exciting in the beginning. A crew, a director, a camera, a script. They're paying you all this money and everyone's nice to you."[20]

Twenty-seven months after beginning her sixty-nine-video porn career, Ginger quit in January 1986, after making *Blame It on Ginger* and *Ginger and Spice*. "I didn't feel good about it. I started doing a lot of drugs, stopped answering my phone, and would go to the mall and spend $10,000."[21]

She studied acting at the Beverly Hills Playhouse and got her first break from an ex-porno director making the action flick *Wild Man*. That led to appearances in *Vice Academy 1, 2,* and *3*. Allen got her Screen Actors Guild card doing *Skin Deep*. "Director Blake Edwards picked me out of a whole group of extras. He said he and his wife [Julie Andrews] enjoyed my work. Imagine! Mary Poppins liked my work!"[22]

Many critics didn't, though. Robb Weller interviewed Ginger for Rona Barrett's *Entertainment This Week* special on "Women in Porn." "No one's going to put a porn queen in any sort of respectable movie," Weller told the March 14, 1986, *Chicago Tribune*. "I don't believe they [porn queens] have much to look forward to. They're trying to say now that in these [porn] films, the woman is in control; she's not beaten and thrown down; it's her fantasies. Hey, there's still no romance, no passion, no love."[23]

Ginger hoped 1993's *Bound and Gagged: A Love Story* would jumpstart her mainstream career. It didn't. As Leslie, the bisexual abused wife, Allen exemplified the trend in B-grade movies to use porn performers as freaks.

Not one to be discouraged, Ginger writes on her internet site about her "blossoming and prolific acting career in mainstream Hollywood films."

◆◆◆◆

Concern over porn moving into the mainstream stimulated investigations by two American presidential commissions. In 1970, the first one (started by Lyndon Baines Johnson) declared sexually explicit entertainment harmless. In 1986, the second commission (created during Ronald Reagan's administration), which was composed mainly of antiporn activists, condemned the industry.

Selling 100,000 copies, mainly to Christians who claimed to be sickened by the large amounts of pornography in the massive document, the 1986 Meese Commission Report featured explicit descriptions of magazines, books, and movies. Liberals cut the report to shreds. The American Civil Liberties Union called the Meese Commission "a national crusade against dirty pictures." Michael Kinsley, writing in the *Wall Street Journal*, called the report "wildly hilarious." A *New York Times* editorial blamed the commissioners for "relying on questionable evidence and recklessly encouraging censorship," and concluded that the report "outruns its own evidence" and that "its cure of censorship is worse than the disease."[24]

Because they disliked its message, mainstream publishers refused to publish the report. For similar reasons, the news media gave the commission little play. The only two reporters who covered the nationwide hearings in their entirety came from *Penthouse Forum*. Along with *Playboy* and other pornographers, *Penthouse* funded an attack on the Meese Commission by the public relations firm Gray & Company, providing three times the entire budget of their target. The efforts were unsuccessful, however, as public opinion and the federal government shifted against the industry.

After the report was released, many pornographers, like Robert McCallum, Paul Ziller, Roberta Findlay, Walter and Gregory Dark, and Hal Freeman, left the medium for such mainstream genres as horror.

"The market for adult films started slipping around 1982," Chuck Vincent told the *Variety*. "In the past three years it's dried up. Five years ago [1983], the video companies such as VCA and Caballero would typically advance $40–60,000 for the video rights to a theatrical porn film. Then two years ago [1986] they stopped making offers—they decided they could do four shot-on-video programs themselves for the cost of video rights to a single theatrical film. These programs are shot in a single day, [and have] no theatrical value."[25]

Screenwriter Rich Marx earned thousands of dollars from his X-rated scripts including *Taboo* but after the video revolution he found himself out of work. He went mainstream. Rich told *Variety* that

> the fundamental difference between now and several years ago is that back then we wanted to make a real picture—which people would enjoy and had possibilities of attracting the crossover, mainstream audience. . . . The new breed are amateurs who have picked up a video camera. Video . . . enabled them to bypass film technique and the entire film distribution business, so they can create a direct-marketing mail-order business to stores and the public, even creating warehouses in their own homes.[26]

Joyce Snyder, who produced the *Raw Talent* series starring Jerry Butler, made the R-rated horror flick *Hazing in Hell* using director Paul Ziller, who had also started in porn. Ziller later directed the straight comedy *Ralph & the Rockets*.

Porn has long served as a training ground for the mainstream. Oscar winner John G. Avildsen directed several X-rated flicks including 1969's *Turn On to Love*, 1970's *Guess What We Learned in School Today?*, and 1971's *Cry Uncle*. Before Scott Cunningham hit it big with *Friday the 13th*, he coproduced and codirected with the late Brad Talbot 1973's porno *Case of the Full Moon Murders*. Gary Graver made more than thirty pornos under the name Robert McCallum. Of all these, however, only David DeCoteau talks freely about his porn past: "I learned everything working in adult films . . . when I started out I had no idea what I was doing . . . but in adult movies, I learned."[27]

Before directing the Oscar-winning documentary *Best Boy*, Ira Wohl edited the 1973 black porno *Lialeh*. John Derek directed and Bo Derek produced but did not appear in the 1978 porno *Love You*, starring Annette Haven. The late Andy Warhol produced, directed, and photographed the sex film *Blue Movie*.

Famous foreign directors who did X include Nagisa Oshima (*In the Realm of the Senses*), Valerian Borowcyk (*La Bête*), and Marco Bellochio (*Devil in the Flesh*), though only Oshima's film contained abundant scenes of penetration. *Playboy* pictorial subject Kristine DeBell, a lifetime star of soap operas and B-movies, performed in the X-rated feature *Alice in Wonderland*.

Unlike directors who tend to stick to one genre, crews move back and forth between porn and the mainstream. "A lot of people in the non-X-rated business pride themselves on never having sunk so low as to make an X-rated picture," says pornographer Ernest Greene. "Anyone who has done hard-core has a lot of resistance and snobbery to overcome. . . . There will never come a time when X-rated videos will be viewed as great, undiscovered gems."[28]

Porn actors also rarely cross to conventional films though Chuck Vincent used many of them in his R-rated projects. "I cast for the best," Vincent told *Variety*, "and adult performers are experienced actors. They suffer because it is difficult for them to escape the connotation of having worked in porn films."[29]

Director Brian DePalma flirted with using Annette

Haven in *Body Double* until studio brass at Columbia nixed her casting because of her porno past. The role went to then little known Melanie Griffith who had learned how to strip on stage from Haven.[30]

Carol Connors (the actress, not the songwriter) appeared in many pornos, including *Deep Throat*, prior to becoming a regular on Chuck Barris's *The Gong Show* TV program. After that, she performed again in such sex films as the *Candy* series. Abigail Clayton switched from porn to costar with Gerard Depardieu in Marco Ferreri's *Bye-Bye, Monkey* and opposite Joe Spinellie in William Lustig's *Maniac*.

The late Wade Nichols (Dennis Parker) made the most successful acting transition. He starred in numerous X-rated films, including *Take Off*, before becoming Detective Mallory in the ABC daytime soap *Edge of the Night*.

Penthouse publisher Bob Guccione used Malcolm McDowell, Sir John Gielgud, and Peter O'Toole in *Caligula*, but they were far away when the Sicilian shot the movie's few explicit scenes. Mainstream author Spaulding Gray appeared in two 1975 porn films—*Farmer's Daughter* and *Misty Beethoven*. Sylvester Stallone appeared naked in 1970's *A Party at Kitty and Stud's*, which features no hardcore action, although there are softcore simulations.

In 1997, a widely distributed videotape displayed explicit sex between actress Pamela Anderson Lee and her rock drummer husband, Tommy Lee. Although the tape was not commercially produced, the Lees knew they were being filmed. Other popular home tapes of celebrity sex feature Rob Lowe, Chuck Barry, and Jayne Kennedy.

To avoid the stigma of porn, most people in the business, cast and crew, use fake names, although a few, such as John Stagliano and Janine Lindemulder, use their real names. Many use something close, such as using their first two real names, but dropping their last name. Ron Jeremy (Hyatt) and Tammi Ann (Fallon) are two examples. Jenna Massoli changed her surname to Jameson. Sarah Sanderson becomes Sahara Sands. Some performers use more than one pseudonym, using names specific to a genre. Al Brown, for example, uses "Peter North" in his straight films and "Matt Ramsey" in his gay films.

Many porn stars copyright their stage names, creating public documents that frequently contain their real name, address, and telephone number. The more famous the performer, the more likely that he or she has left a paper trail.

"The Mother Lode of porn star real names is the Los Angeles County's registry of Fictitious Business Names," writes lawyer N. P. Trist, an assumed name. "The files go back for decades and contain information on long-retired stars of the '70s and '80s. Porn stars who use this service tend to register their stage names (Lauren Pokorny registered 'Porsche Lynn') or the names of their fan clubs (Kathleen M. Runco registered 'Leena's Fan Club')."[31]

There are ways for a porn star to keep her real name private. "And in a few years," Trist says, "once I am a practicing attorney, I will gladly tell you how and make it so. For $125 an hour."[32]

❖❖❖❖

During these dark days of harassment and declining product quality, the arrival of a gentleman publisher and a friendly court decision helped the industry achieve spectacular growth in the 1990s.

With the explosion of publicity about porn because of Traci Lords and the Meese Commission, the news media sought an accurate source of information about the adult industry. It wasn't easy to find. Porn has never produced either good writing or good journalism. Pornographers usually do best when anonymous. The more the public finds out about the business, the more their fears are confirmed.

During the mid to late 1980s, the news media found that the best of a bad bunch of sources about porn was a new magazine started by a Philadelphia college writer named Paul Fishbein, who'd been winning journalism awards since he was fifteen.

"It was predetermined that I was going to be publishing a magazine," says Fishbein. "When I wasn't doing my magazine in college, I edited the entertainment section of the *Temple News* [college paper]. I've always written well and been interested in publishing. I even put mock magazines together when I wasn't publishing a real magazine."[33]

While in college, Fishbein worked at a video store, where he and a friend who was a writer came up with the idea of creating a newsletter on the adult entertainment industry. "People kept coming up to me at the store and asking me to recommend an adult tape," Fishbein explains, "and I kept saying, 'This one rents well and this one rents well.' I had seen eight adult movies at that time in my entire life."[34]

The pair realized that consumers new to porn knew little or nothing about adult films, so the newsletter was geared toward them. When subscriptions began coming in from video store owners, they learned that even retailers needed to be told which were good films. Thus, the newsletter was changed to a trade publication*: *Adult Video News* (*AVN*).

A typical issue of *AVN* contains an editorial section consisting of industry news, reviews, and gossip, as well as

---

*A trade publication is one written for the industry rather than for general readers.

analyses of various issues affecting the industry. The bulk of any given issue, however, is comprised of advertisements.

"*Adult Video News* hit its stride at the expense of everyone else in the industry," says Fishbein. "During the Meese Commission and major federal raids [on pornographers] during the Reagan and Bush administrations, we became a source for major information."[35]

When the news media wanted accurate information on the adult video industry, they began turning to Fishbein and *Adult Video News.*

Porn critic Pat Riley is a favorite target of Fishbein's magazine. "And some of its reviewers hate my guts," says Riley, because he won't toe the party line.[36] As an example, Riley lists a number of myths about the industry perpetrated by *AVN* and other industry shills:

1. Porno manufacturers produce a quality product. Riley believes that 99 percent of today's porn is garbage.
2. Performers are actresses and actors. "That's an insult to any stage or regular movie actor. Twenty years old and a couple of years shaking the booty in a nudie bar doesn't make an actress," Riley says.
3. Performers are all gorgeous. In Riley's opinion, there are and have ever been only a few who could compete with the level of beauty of the runway models.
4. Female performers orgasm on screen. Riley says no way.
5. The girls want sex with the men. Riley doesn't think so: "If there wasn't any money, no sex would take place."[37]

In the mid- to late 1980s, an antipornography initiative by the Los Angeles County district attorney's office backfired.

The district attorney's prosecution of adult video producer Harold Freeman led to a California Supreme Court ruling in 1989 that effectively legalized production of porn.

In 1982 California changed its antipimping law to mandate a minimum three-year sentence if a defendant were found guilty of "pandering," the legal term for pimping. Democratic state senator David A. Roberti designed the legislation to reduce the street prostitution that bothered his Hollywood district. Although the law's intent was to combat street-walking, the Los Angeles County district attorney's office decided to use it against several producers of hardcore videos.

The district attorney claimed that the exchange of money for sex equaled prostitution, regardless of whether the sex was filmed. The DA hoped that if the law was enforced, California would cease to be the world capital of porn movies.

Harold Freeman, a veteran producer of more than one hundred adult videos, was the first person charged. In September 1983, the forty-seven-year-old Freeman shot the anal-themed *Caught from Behind 2* in Rancho Palos Verdes, a suburb south of Los Angeles. Freeman was charged with five counts of pandering, one count for each woman whom he paid to perform in the film. He was not charged for paying the male performers or for obscenity.

After a six-day jury trial in Van Nuys Superior Court, Freeman was found guilty on all counts. However, the trial judge refused to sentence Freeman to the mandatory three years on the grounds that such a sentence would be cruel and unusual punishment. Instead, Freeman got ninety days in jail, a $10,000 fine, and five years' probation.

Freeman's attorneys filed a routine appeal to the California Supreme Court, which, like most higher courts, denies requests for appeal on many of the cases filed. But four justices of the California Supreme Court decided Freeman's case was worthy of review. After submission of briefs and oral arguments, the court threw out Freeman's conviction and explicitly legalized production of hardcore. "The prosecution of defendant under the pandering statute must be viewed as a transparent attempt at an 'end run' around the First Amendment and obscenity laws," wrote Justice Kaufman. "The self-evident purpose of the prosecuting authority in bringing these charges was to prevent profiteering in pornography without the necessity of proving obscenity."[38]

Pornographers in southern California now pick up production permits at the same government office that certifies shoots for Disney.

Notes

1. Personal interview with Jim South, May 1996.

2. *Fallen Angels*, documentary directed by Bruce Behan, produced by Vestron, 1985.

3. Ibid.

4. Ibid.

5. Ibid.

6. Ibid.

7. Ibid.

8. Ibid.

9. Personal interview with Bill Margold, March 1996.

10. Pat Jordan, "Traci Lords with Her Clothes On," *GQ*, (April 1990): 250.

11. Ibid.

12. Paul Feldman and Ronald L. Soble, "Sex Film Star Not Facing Charges," *Los Angeles Times*, July 19, 1986.

13. Jordan, "Traci Lords," p. 252.

14. Susan Chenery, "After the Fall," *Sydney Morning Herald*, July 15, 1995.

15. Michael Louis Albo, "Alexandra Quinn," *Hustler Erotic Video Guide* (November 1996): 45.

16. Ibid.

17. Ibid.

18. Carol Lynn Mithers, "She Works Hard for the Money: Portrait of a Porn Star," *Mademoiselle* (November 1985): 172.

19. Jerry Butler, *Raw Talent* (Amherst, N.Y.: Prometheus Books, 1990), p. 123.

20. Mithers, "She Works Hard for the Money."

21. Ibid.

22. Ibid.

23. Michael Sneed and Kathy O'Malley, "Rob and Ginger and Rona," *Chicago Tribune*, March 14, 1986.

24. Terry Teachout, "The Pornography Report That Never Was," *Commentary* (August 1987): 51.

25. Lawrence Cohn, "Pornmakers Surface in Mainstream," *Variety* (March 9, 1988): 3.

26. Ibid., p. 26.

27. Ibid.

28. Robert Stoller and Ira Levine, *Coming Attractions* (New Haven, Conn.: Yale University Press, 1993).

29. Cohn, "Pornmakers Surface."

30. Ibid.

31. Quoted from an essay posted on the Internet newsgroup alt.sex.movies at http://home.eznet.net/~rwilhelm/asm/library/misc/real-names-faq.html. The essay by "N. P. Trist" was originaly posted on the newsgroup alt.sex.movies (ASM) February 2, 1996.

32. Ibid.

33. Personal interview with Paul Fishbein, June 1996.

34. Ibid.

35. Ibid.

36. Quoted from a post by Pat Riley to the Internet newsgroup rec.arts.movies.erotica (RAME), August 1997.

37. Ibid.

38. *People* v. *Freeman*, 46 Cal. 3d 419, 758; P.2d 1128, 250 Cal. Rptr. 598 (1989). Quoted by "N. P. Trist" in his essay "Why Porn Is Legal in California," posted to ASM October 13, 1995. Located in the ASM library at http://home.eznet.net/~rwilhelm/asm/library/essays/porn-legal-ca.html.

9.

Analities

After a ten-year layoff, black and interracial porn returned in 1983, produced chiefly for the white porn consumer. "That more blacks have been viewing this material is purely accidental," says Bill Margold, who made 1983's *Hot Chocolate*. "When I put blacks in my videos, I project my fantasies, not theirs."[1] According to veteran prosecutor Bruce Taylor, who loves to seat blacks on his juries, "porn is a white man's disease."[2]

"The porn industry grinds in the most pejorative views of blacks it can find (all those ghetto movies)," writes Pat Riley on the Internet newsgroup RAME (rec.arts.movies.erotica). "Pornographers perpetuate the stereotypical view of a shiftless, just-out-of-prison, socially maladapted group. [Racism in porn] . . . is not some [white] actress who doesn't want to screw a black guy (for whatever reason) but a concerted attempt by the producers to appeal to the basest elements of the viewing population."[3]

African American Angel Kelly racked up 150 X-rated

videos, performing every type of sex but anal. Earning up to
$1,000 a day, she worked continuously from 1986 through
the end of 1987, making several hundred thousand dollars.
Kelly's porn stardom helped her stripping career, which
brought in up to $4,000 a week.[4]

Angel Kelly had grown up poor in Michigan, the only
black in the crowd of rich kids she hung with. After a dis-
agreement with her mother, she quit school and left home.
She worked as a runway model for six months and taught a
dance class to such students as porn star Porsche Lynn.

The black girl entered the sex industry at age nineteen by
masturbating behind a glass partition in a private booth while
men put money in a slot and jacked off. Kelly kept all the
money, but the six months of men ejaculating against the
glass partition changed her. "I began to look cheaper and
sleazier. . . . I began to see men in their truest form and they
are unbelievably sick."[5]

Kelly never loses an opportunity to claim victim status,
such as in an interview for the November 1988 issue of
Essence. "It's hard to be an adult actress in the business, especially if you're black. The industry looks upon us performers
with such disgust. I've never been recognized with awards
and magazine covers. Black women are hired to play hookers
and maids, and I've never earned residuals. Sometimes companies put sex scenes I've done in one video into a com-
pletely different video, and I've never earned a dime on
them."[6] What she doesn't mention is that virtually no X performer earns residuals, and neither have other performers
received payment for multiple uses of footage.

Kelly says her past haunts her. Some men won't date her
because she used to work in the sex business. "Even after I'm
dead, my videos will be out there. I've been swallowed up by
the adult video industry. I feel used and cheated."[7]

Kelly's experience with porn was so horrible that she returned to the business in 1996.

By 1998, porn boasted a handful of black girls under contract to various production companies—Heather Hunter with Vivid, Brooke Harlow with Metro, and Midori with Video Team. They usually earn about half the wages of their white counterparts, mostly because their productions do not sell as well. Sex vids with interracial sex are usually low-budget affairs that rarely appear on cable TV.

Porn's leading black male, Sean Michaels, moved from Brooklyn to Los Angeles in 1989. "A trained actor who also has the face and figure of a male model," writes porn journalist Jeremy Stone, "plus the X-rated bonus of being well-hung—Sean is a welcome addition to the too thin ranks of talented male performers."[8]

Michaels has appeared in about 600 videos and he also directs many of the best black and interracial features on the market. The actor's main drawback as a performer is his meager spew—the result of a vasectomy. "Part of the fun of watching pornography is the chance of an interracial pregnancy," porn fan "Ira" writes on RAME. "The idea of a sterile male star is almost as disgusting as a female star with a boob job."[9]

Many white girls won't work with Michaels because of his skin color, and producers tend to avoid him and other black performers in their big-budget productions.* Michaels has done great scenes, such as one with Ashlyn Gere, that were later redone with a white actor because of distributors' reluctance to move top sex vids with interracial sex.

---

*According to many pornographers, the following porn stars categorically refused, at one time or another, to work with anyone black: Julia Ann, Barbara Dare, Racquel Darrien, Jenna Jameson, Hyapatia Lee, Traci Lords, Ginger Lynn, Savannah, Samantha Strong, and Tori Welles.

Despite the stigma against interracial sex, for years, Michaels avoided sex on camera with black girls.

His fight against discrimination frequently produces addled products, such as 1993's *Erotica*. "With an opening title that reads, 'From the imagination of Sean Michaels,' on down to the quotes pleading for racial unity credited to him," writes *AFW*, "Sean has lost his mind—or owns a synthetic version of a Spike Lee/Madonna meld."[10]

Pat Riley loathed Michaels's *Butts Afire*. "Sean Michaels, who is responsible for the concept and dialogue, has just replaced Paul Thomas at the top of my list of most hated directors. . . . I used to think that Sean was a competent porn actor who just happened to have a black skin but now he . . . preaches to the audience. . . . Michaels confuses anti-black discrimination with anti-ugly discrimination. . . . To raise the quality of this movie, get rid of [actresses] Toy and Domonique with their horrible bodies."[11]

Racism flows through porn. Only whites and part-Asians such as Asia Carrera show up in the big-budget productions that end up in modified forms on cable. Cable companies generally won't show interracial sex because it upsets many of their conservative customers, such as hotels in the South. "Blacks don't go over in the South," says one pornographer. "That's a big piece of the market. Black girls, yes, as long as they aren't dominant, just women who are fucked."[12] Because of this bias, when blacks show up in porn, the title of the video usually announces it, as in *Black Beauty* and *Black Velvet*.

Porn's leading white beauties receive warnings from powerful pornographers to avoid blacks, whether on screen, stripping, or in personal life. If white missy doesn't toe this racial line, she's supposedly regarded as white trash.

Many black male performers, such as Devlin Weed, Tony

Everready, Byron Long, and Jimmy Z. appear unpleasant, thus providing little incentive for leading white girls to do them. The impressions are reinforced by productions like Ron Hightower's *White Chick* series, which features black guys talking about their latest prison stints and how they plan to fuck white bitches.

No black has ever competed with the star power of an Ashlyn Gere or Christy Canyon. No black ranks among the industry's one hundred all-time leading performers. Producers don't hire black women for box covers—except for so-called specialty tapes with "black" in the title.

Porn excellence, like all forms of excellence, depends on discrimination. Pornographers discriminate against the old, tired, and ugly, against directors who lose money and those who rock the boat. Just as professional sports discriminate against those not athletically gifted, pornographers discriminate against those not aesthetically gifted. Until the 1970s, pro sports allowed its prejudice against blacks to overwhelm its desire for excellence. Some 1990s pornographers' desire for excellence may be similarly overwhelmed by their prejudice against darker skin color.

Because porn is a free market with ease of entry and exit, the dearth of quality black productions indicates either discrimination at the highest levels of distribution (e.g., General Video) or that there is little demand for such product.

❖❖❖❖

During the final days of the twentieth century, writes author R. A. Lafferty, popular culture turns less to eschatology, the study of final things, than to analities, the study of rear end things.

Back in 1983, porn verged on respectability, with directors like Chuck Vincent telling sensitive stories about relationships. The forces of darkness quickly re-enveloped the industry, however. Directors Bruce "Seven" Behan, Hal Freeman, and Greg Dark found success through exploring the human's dirtiest parts.

Dark debuted with *Let Me Tell Ya 'Bout White Chicks*. The nihilistic filmmaker did more than anyone to change the direction of porn to the nasty and anal and to change fans' selection criteria from primarily seeking a star performer to frequently seeking a star director—be it Dark, John Stagliano, Bruce Behan, or John Leslie.

Walter "Dark" Gernert, a rich kid turned pornographer, served as Greg Dark's producer until 1993. They made 1984's *New Wave Hookers*, the most influential porn video of the last quarter century next to *The Adventures of Buttman*. "Two low-lifes—Jamie Gillis and Jack Baker—dream up a call girl ring where the whores turn tricks to new wave music," writes *AFW*. "The ultimate Dark Brothers movie combines humor, stylized sets, and a rich variety of editing styles."[13]

Other Dark Brothers (both men are white) material includes *Blackthroat*, in which Erica Boyer lives out her screen name as Double Penetration Slut. "The Dark Brothers don't make tapes for the couples market," writes Bob Rimmer. "Show this one to most women and they won't laugh. But there's another kind of market of guys in fraternities and horny old men in their lodges who will probably watch this in total awe, and may even chuckle at the insanity."[14]

Blackthroat appeared in 1985 and featured its own rock music with the chorus, "You're gonna see black heads sucking on white heads and white heads sucking on black heads." Reflecting his personal experience, Dark usually portrays blacks as morons.[15]

Between the Cheeks 2 explores the psychosexual world of a mental patient who has delusions of being a pimp. Believing the soul is found in the colon, he fears that aliens want to enter us through our asses. Salvation lies in not defecating.

Following in the footsteps of Gerard Damiano, Dark appears obsessed with sin and punishment, particularly his *Creasemaster* series, *New Wave Hookers 3*, and *The Devil in Miss Jones 3–5.* His videos produce shocking and unerotic images of, for example, a naked fat lady (in *Flesh*), that seem designed to punish viewers for the sin of using pornography. "*New Wave Hookers* is often unerotic," notes Jim Holliday, "which is Gregory Dark's purpose—to slap America across the face and to explore new depths of depravity."[16]

The argument that Dark intends to punish his viewers is reinforced by the synopsis of *The Devil in Miss Jones 4*, which he sent to reviewers in advance of the tape:

> Justine Jones (Lois Ayres) realizes she's never going to get out of hell unless she blows Cerberus (Kevin James). Swallowing her pride, along with a little jism, Justine gives Cerberus the best skull he's ever had. Negro (Jack Baker) looks on. Moving down, Justine and Negro descend into the Perverse Room. . . . Negro leads Justine down to his favorite room in hell, the Racists' Room, . . . where dead racists are forced to have sex with their most hated ethnic groups. A dominant Black Chick (Purple Passion) punishes an American Nazi member as two Zulu Warriors (Robbie Dee, FM Bradley) double penetrate a lily white Southern Belle (Patti Petite) while Justine looks on in shock.

Stopping many masturbators in mid-stroke, Dark's productions such as *Devil in Miss Jones 3–5* do not make for pleasant viewing. They are far nastier, for instance, than Ron Sullivan's hilarious *Devil in Miss Jones 2*.

"I do my own thing," says Dark. "I want to make nasty, wild, hardcore sex, but I also want to . . . examine what sex is. I constantly try to shock the audience. I don't want people to ever know what they're going to see in my movies. Like a carnival—a freak show."[17]

AVN praises the themes and methods Dark and other such directors embrace. Since the concept hit big in the 1980s, anal-themed sex vids have been sure sellers. "Forget about clever dialogue and expensive sets and concentrate on these three-ways, foot fetish scenes, dildo action, and rear-end action," the reviewers write.[18] "Sex in America has to be nasty," says Rimmer, "[It is] a leftover from Saint Thomas Aquinas's belief that it's 'the union of two sewer systems.' "[19]

John Stagliano's *The Adventures of Buttman* (1989) changed the direction of porn more than any other production in the history of the genre. Until *Buttman*, most pornographers, no matter how low the budget, tried to make a movie. Stagliano took the camera off the tripod and pioneered the gonzo style that dominates video porn at the end of the twentieth century.

A series of loops that connect in an odd way, *The Adventures of Buttman* returned porn to its stag past. *Buttman* "starts melodramatically," writes *Adam Film World*, "then it becomes the cameraman's story. . . . This is a sensuous feature. Few pornos are."[20]

Porn's leading sodomist—and misogynist—is the sadistic but charming Paul Little, better known by his porn name Max Hardcore. His reputation is as vicious as his videos, and although his movies, in which he acts as well as directs, are frequently cutting edge, the beauty of the females is frequently below par because the best looking girls won't perform with him. Hardcore sex can be a full-contact sport like football. Max claims that he fucks women so hard that several ended up in the hospital with internal bleeding, torn ligaments, and other injuries.[21]

After high school, Max worked construction and fashion photography. He moved to California in 1990 with his older brother, met producer Bobby Hollander, and produced scenes for the most popular amateur line of the time—*Mr. Peepers*. Max credits Hollander for teaching him the vignette "pro-am" formula of using amateur and professional performers in a mix of four to five stories per tape. Ron Sullivan taught Max to use language during a sex scene instead of canned music.

Zane Entertainment distributed the series that made Max famous—*The Anal Adventures of Max Hardcore*, which debuted in 1992. Later that year Hardcore launched *Cherry Poppers*, featuring women over eighteen years of age dressed as young girls. "The industry flipped out," says Hardcore, "but now you see half-a-dozen series that imitate *Cherry Poppers*."[22]

As Hardcore's popularity zoomed, he gained control of his product, creating Filmwest Productions in late 1994. His latest releases include *MAX*, *Max World*, *Hardcore Schoolgirls*, *Maxed Out*, and *Anal Auditions*. These films include several porn "trademarks" that were Max's own innovations:

- techniques that open up a girl's anus or vagina to gaping proportions.
- throatfucking, where Max takes the girl by the hair and reams her throat with his cock.
- splatter cam—a camera placed under a girl with a shield over the lens. The girl's and Max's splatter onto the camera. "It lets the viewer feel he's lying under the action."
- speculum—an instrument used by doctors to open up a woman's vagina during a gynecological examination. Max uses a clear, plexiglass version.

Numerous pornographers copy Max Hardcore's techniques—such as Jay Ashley, Al Borda, and Robert Black—but they don't do it right. "They're clumsy and awkward," says Max, "like children trying to assemble a toy for the first time."[23]

"Max Hardcore is Maximum Hardcore," says Bill Margold. "He keeps porn in the gutter where it belongs. Max Hardcore eats, drinks, and thinks sex and pours it right back out through his camera lens."[24]

"Regardless of how disgusted many of you are by Max's current behavior," porn fan Jack Koff writes on the newsgroup RAME (rec.arts.movies.erotica), "he is the most influential and important director of the '90s."[25] Before Max, porn videos used lame plots and little anal sex. The new porn world of gonzo overflows with all-anal videos, and "backdoor sex" seems particularly nasty because the rectum is better designed for expulsion than penetration. During anal intercourse, thin rectal skin layers tend to chafe and bleed, and although women porn stars usually take enemas to clean themselves out before filming, the scenes still tend to get messy.

During the 1980s, anal sex was done with sensitivity. The anal of the 1990s, however, "aims to humiliate the girl as much as possible," writes Koff. "This is where Max has had his greatest impact upon porn. Before Max there was no such thing as closeups of dilated assholes, constant insults and name calling, . . . repeated ass to mouth penetration without a cut [in the film], the 'cherry poppers' routine."[26]

"The Max Hardcore series has become nauseating," writes Bob Rimmer in his review of *The Anal Adventures of Max Hardcore: Suzy Superslut.*

But my guess is that's why they're big sellers—not for sexual turn-ons but for gasps of horror at sights you've never seen before. The Asian gal not only deepthroats his cock, but gets her tongue into Max's asshole, and the extended buggering of her poop-shute [*sic*] along with a dildo shoved in her vagina, or the scenes where Max finger fucks their vagina walls with his finger inserted in their anuses are not for the squeamish. Before you're through, you'll have had all the "up the ass" you need in a life-time.[27]

"In his pickup phase," writes *AVN*, "Max is undeniably charming, with a patented non-threatening persona. When we get to the sex, especially the rough fingering and rough language . . . this is a mutual exploration of the sexual edges with Max the foul-mouthed, experienced guide."[28]

◆◆◆◆

Few discussions of porn, particularly anal porn, go ten min-utes without bringing up the subject of AIDS. For years, the mainstream media and the politically correct element in X-rated entertainment issued apocalyptic warnings that virtu-ally every performer in the industry would contract HIV, the AIDS virus, and die. One example is an article in the first issue of *Men's Perspective*, which claims, "It's a small miracle that the entire industry isn't already HIV positive."[29] *Vanity Fair* was even more emphatic: "In the age of AIDS, nothing could be more crazily chancy than the multiple-partner unsafe sex practiced by porn stars (who are also often sub-stance abusers and/or bi). The Meese Commission may not have to make a move. The porn industry seems intent on sodomizing itself into extinction."[30]

Ona Zee, a veteran of over one thousand sexvids, spoke in the same tone. "The industry doesn't want to know about this question. They are wearing blinders and hoping, praying that nothing happens."[31]

Contrary to this rhetoric, American pornographers take more care to protect themselves and their employees than pornographers in Europe, Asia, and the rest of the world. American performers get HIV tests every month and must present a copy of the negative result before working. Companies like Vivid and VCA frequently use condoms on their shoots at a significant cost to sales and profits—"The vast majority of male porn viewers do not want to see condoms in explicit movies," as Jim Holliday notes.[32]

Though they make sex safer, condoms ruin masturbatory dreams. Critic Pat Riley, for instance, loves the

> fantasy of getting the girl pregnant—the most erotic thing in the world—and if you show a condom, the visible chances of her getting pregnant are close to nil. . . . All those who like facials out of hostility to the female are babes in the wood when it comes to controlling and degrading the female. By making her pregnant you're controlling her reproduction. . . . Cum on her face can be wiped off in an instant; it's tougher to get rid of an embryo. . . . If she doesn't [have an abortion], it's nine months of morning sickness, bloating, clothes that won't fit, difficulty sitting down, getting up, birth . . .[33]

While over one hundred homosexual performers in homo-porn have died of AIDS, no exclusively heterosexual male in hetero-porn has died of AIDS.[34] As is the case throughout the Western world, porn's AIDS cases demonstrate that HIV does discriminate: Gays and intravenous drug users are far more likely to get it than straights and women are more likely to be HIV-positive than men. During the 1990s, at least eight females and two males in the heterosexual porn industry have tested HIV-positive.[35]

From AIDS to the Mob, the specter of death has long haunted porn. Shauna Grant, a 1982 discovery of Bobby

Hollander, blew her brains out in 1984. Other porn star suicides include Melba Brue, Mary Millington, Talia James, Lynn Tars, Tina Ross, Wade Nichols, Savannah, Megan Leigh, Nancee Kellee, Alex Jordan, and Cal Jammer. Laurien Dominique choked to death. Kathy Harcout was fished out of New York's East River. Tiffany Lane died in a car accident that result in the amputation of one of Patti Petite's legs. Veri Knotty, transsexual Jill Munro, Michael Bruce, Kevin James, and Danny Husong all died young. Linda Wong, Arcadia Lake, and about a dozen other performers died of drug overdoses. A john murdered female performer Charli Waters in 1989. Six years later, a wave knocked director Michael Ricaud off a cliff and to his death during a shoot. European porn actor Riny Rey was gunned down in Budapest on April 12, 1996, just days after finishing work on *Private Dancer* and *Sin*, two productions for Private. In 1997, a shootout at porn production company Elegant Angel killed pornographer Israel Gonzalez and one cop. About a dozen gay performers have killed themselves, including Joel Curry, Christian Fox, Fred Halstead, and Alan Lambert.[36]

❖❖❖❖

Fem porn. Those two words in a 100,000-word book on porn are about as much coverage as the genre earns through sales. But in these politically correct times, one must waste space to deal with myths.

Historically limited to one half of the population, producers seek the Holy Grail of "couples porn," a mythical form of sexually explicit entertainment that attracts as many female buyers as men. That it doesn't exist doesn't stop those with an agenda from seeking it. Like Jews waiting for the Messiah and Christians for the Second Coming, porn reviewers like *AVN* and producers like Vivid seek salvation through feminine porn, an oxymoron.

When magazines such as *AVN* use terms like "fem porn" or "couples films," they refer to X-rated videos with less raunch and more dialogue and character development than most. More talk and less cum. More story and less cunt. "Pornography made by women tends to be prettier (nicer photography, fewer hairy men wearing grimy socks)," writes Maitland McDonagh in her excellent book *The 50 Most Erotic Films*. Women "pay more attention to narrative—how the bodies get into bed together rather than just what they do once they get there."[37] Examples of this softer porn range from the production company Vivid to actress Candida Royalle.

"Fem porn" receives publicity out of proportion to its popularity because, if ever created, it would bring more dollars for pornographers (which is why they promote it) and more ammunition for ideologues (which is why the liberal media loves it). If porn sold to women as much as to men, producers like VCA and Vivid would double their gross. And commercially viable porn for women would tilt the significance of nurture over nature in the psychosexual makeup of males and females, erasing what appear to be painful differences between the sexes.

"It's a nice idea to have women erotica stars as directors," reads *The Couples Guide to the Best Erotic Videos*, "but we can't say that their day jobs have made them any better, or given them more insight into the making of an erotic tape."[38]

Porn belongs solely to males masturbating. Go to any sex shop and you'll rarely see a woman, because women rarely masturbate to sexually explicit pictures of strangers. Though there are thousands of sex magazines for men, there's only one for women—*Playgirl*—and mainly gay men buy it. Couples films "appeal to squeamish suburbanites seeking a walk on the wild side without getting their shoes dirtied," writes *Hustler Erotic Video Guide*'s Mike Albo. "Lots of lingering, longing glances heavy with 'meaning,' sappy muzak, and no cum shots. Femme films like *Christine's Secret, Three Daughters*, and *Sensual Escape* are the porn equivalents of Harlequin Romance novels."[39]

Female contributions to creating porn are negligible, although their names appear frequently in the producing and directing credits. Several male pornographers use female names, such as Jane Waters (John Keeler), Judy Blue (Paul Thomas), and Loretta Sterling (Ed deRoo). Much ballyhooed female "pornographers" such as Gail Palmer left the real work to directors like Bob Chinn and Robert McCallum. If no woman had ever directed a porno, the medium would be essentially unchanged, say such leading female directors as Jane Hamilton. Porn's most productive women, such as Hamilton, Patti Rhodes, Teresa Orlowski, and Gail Force, usually align themselves with men.

Pornographers routinely exaggerate female contributions to counter the criticism that porn exploits women and to enable men to persuade their female partners to watch a dirty film. For example, Carlos Tobalina's wife, Maria Pia (who knew virtually nothing about making movies), served as president of the Adult Film Association. The smut media gladly participate in these deceptions, as do many male viewers.

Notes

1. Personal interview with Bill Margold, March 1996.
2. Personal interview with Bruce Taylor, June 1997.

3. Pat Riley Internet post to RAME (rec.arts.movies. erotica), June 1997.

4. Bebe Campbell, "A Portrait of Angel," *Essence* (November 1990): 250.

5. Ibid.

6. Ibid.

7. Ibid.

8. "Sean Michaels," *Adam Film World 1996 Directory*, p. 42.

9. Post to RAME, July 1997.

10. *Adam Film World 1997 Directory*, p. 259.

11. Robert Rimmer and Pat Riley, *X-Rated Videotape Guide IV* (Amherst, N.Y.: Prometheus Books, 1996), p. 172.

12. "Blacks in Porn," *Adam Film World* (June 1983): 24.

13. *Adam Film World 1996 Directory*, p. 261.

14. Robert Rimmer, *X-Rated Videotape Guide* (Amherst, N.Y.: Prometheus Books, 1993), p. 336.

15. Personal interviews with Greg Dark, March 1996.

16. Jim Holliday, *Only the Best* (Van Nuys, Calif.: Cal Vista Direct Ltd., 1986).

17. Dark interview.

18. "Virgin Cheeks," *Adult Video News 1997 Entertainment Guide*, p. 267.

19. Rimmer, *X-Rated Videotape Guide*, p. 336.

20. *Adam Film World 1996 Directory*, p. 247.

21. Nick Ravo, "The Core of Paul Little," *Icon* (February 1997): 100–109.

22. Personal interview with Paul Little, March 1997.

23. Ibid.

24. Margold interview.

25. Jack Koff Internet post to RAME, July 1997.

26. Ibid.

27. Rimmer and Riley, *X-Rated Videotape Guide IV*, p. 45.

28. "Max Hardcore 10: High Voltage," *Adult Video News* (February 1995): 134.

29. "The Porno Plague," *Men's Perspective*, issue 1 (1996): 145.

30. James Wolcott, "A Walk on the Dark Side," *Vanity Fair* (March 1987): 30–31.

31. Quoted in "The Porno Plague," p. 145.

32. Jim Holliday, "Oh Boy, Oh Joy, Another Gang Bang Movie," *Adult Video News* (September 1996): 68.

33. Pat Riley Internet post to RAME, July 1997.

34. Luke Ford, "AIDS," posted on http://www.lukeford. com/d63.html (July 1998).

35. Ibid.

36. Luke Ford, "Dead Porn Stars," posted on http://www. lukeford.com/d46.html (January 1999). See also Heidenry, *What Wild Ecstasy*, p. 240.

37. Maitland McDonagh, *The 50 Most Erotic Films of All Time* (New York: Citadel Press, 1996), p. xv.

38. Steve and Elizabeth Brent, *Couples Guide to the Best Erotic Videos* (New York: St. Martin's Press, 1997), p. 88.

39. Quoted in Luke Ford, "Fem Porn," posted on http:// www.lukeford.com/64.html (October 1997).

10.

Porn in the 1990s

During the 1980s, porn retreated under the aggressive assault of federal investigators, Christians, and feminists. Leading pornographers such as Gregory Dark and Hal Freeman left the medium to work for mainstream independent filmmakers. Leading mobsters such as Robert DiBernardo were murdered. Shooting on film virtually ceased. During 1988 and 1989, the X-Rated Critics Organization (XRCO) chose to give no award for Best Film due to the paucity of product. Circulation of sex magazines such as *Penthouse* plunged when the 7–11 Corporation, pressured by the Meese Commission, decided to stop selling the magazines in their convenience stores. From 1988 to 1989, X-rated tape rentals fell by 3 million to 395 million, a number which comprised 12 percent of all rentals, porn's lowest percentage ever.[1] Following the 1986 Meese Commission Report, federal agents traveled to the Bible Belt to seek obscenity convictions. By 1992, twenty pornographers had been convicted. Many went to jail and others paid millions of dollars in fines. "It's a holocaust," complained porn attorney John Weston, who accused the government of seeking to destroy "an entire genre" of entertainment.[2]

"The legal battles . . . are just the latest problems to beset the porn business," wrote the *Los Angeles Times* on February 17, 1991. "After a period of 'porn chic,' in the early '70s, when hip couples went to X-rated theaters to see *The Devil in Miss Jones* the way New York dilettantes used to go to the Cotton Club in Harlem, pornography has lost its eclat. Twenty years after *Deep Throat* helped bring the grimy sex film out of the closet, it is no longer cool to be seen waiting in line with the raincoat crowd at an X-rated theater."[3]

Amid much government and citizen harassment, pornographers since the late 1980s have chiefly blamed one of their own for their declining profits—Mark Carriere. Using the name Mark Curtis, Carriere shot numerous videos during the early 1980s, including *Hollywood Heartbreakers*.

Born in 1949, Carriere grew up in Merrillville, Indiana. He entered porn in the early 1980s with his younger brother Brad, who became his treasurer. Debuting at approximately the same time as high-end producer Vivid Video, the Carrieres flooded the market with cheap product.

"I'm always looking to cut corners, to cut people out of the picture," Carriere told the *Los Angeles Times*.[4] He said his sales rose from $3 million a year in 1985 to $30 million in 1990. The soft-spoken, shaggy-haired newcomer profited from the talents of a veteran: Ron Jeremy. "I was the king of killer and filler," remembers Jeremy, "all these techniques of hiring that one girl who's on the boxcover and shooting her for two or three scenes and then make two or three movies using her. The next day we'd shoot the filler—the girls who were less expensive, and then we'd have three movies. It was a conveyor belt style of moviemaking."[5]

Jeremy and Carriere didn't invent the one-day wonder, but as far as profits were concerned, they perfected the medium. In 1980 porn videotapes sold for $100. By 1990, many tapes sold brand new for $5. Carriere and his corner-cutting production methods may not have caused the plunge, but he probably made more money from it than anyone.

Unable to compete, veteran production companies Caballero and Western Visuals experienced severe cash flow problems and never recovered. Nor did Teddy Snyder, who had begun by shooting loops in New York in the late 1960s, including several starring Eric Edwards and Linda Lovelace. After moving to Los Angeles in 1980 with fellow New Yorkers Bobby Hollander and Bobby Genova, Snyder formed a series of production companies including Video Cassette Recordings (VCR). He produced such schlock as the compilation tapes *Screaming Desire* and *Naked Night*. As the porn business turned downward in the late 1980s, Snyder made inept ventures into distributing educational tapes for children, frequently mistakenly placing porn tapes into children's box covers.[6]

In early 1989, Snyder, a vial of cocaine in his hand, was gunned down on his front lawn in what looked like a Mafia-style hit. His wife, Sharon, was later tried and found not guilty of hiring the assassin. Three months pregnant at the time of the hit, Sharon said her husband wanted to leave porn because his customers didn't buy enough. "Maybe people aren't as perverted as we thought."[7]

❖❖❖❖

In 1990, federal prosecutors called Harry Mohney the nation's second-largest purveyor of pornography and estimated his net worth at more than $100 million with a financial interest in more than 100 cabarets, peep shows, movie theaters, and bookstores in fifteen states.[8]

In 1991, Mohney began serving three years in prison for tax evasion. The government successfully argued that Mohney used "a complex veil of deceit" to conceal his ownership in the businesses, including a network of sham corporations and front men, and that the money he skimmed from the operations "provided (Mohney) with an untaxed, virtually untraceable cash trove of nearly $1 million a year." Mohney's "utter lack of remorse and denial of responsibility is merely further evidence of his contempt for the law when it does not suit his needs."[9]

Mohney's most significant contribution to the sex industry is the development of "gentlemen's clubs"—upper class strip joints. He saw back in 1970 that the big money lay not in seedy bookstores and peepshows but in glittering bars featuring nude dancers. Often called the Howard Hughes of porn, Mohney now owns and operates the Déjà Vu strip club chain which brings him and his partners over $10 million a year.[10]

Americans now spend more money at strip clubs than at plays, opera, ballet, and classical music performances combined. The growth of sex videos during the 1990s coincided with the opening of large gentlemen's clubs across the country. Top porn actresses earn up to $20,000 a week by performing several twenty-minute shows each evening. These strippers, known as "feature dancers," largely get paid according to their appearances in hardcore videos, video box-covers, and magazine spreads. In the hierarchy of sex workers, strippers once looked down on porn stars. Now they compete for roles in hardcore.[11]

Although porn taps into insatiable desires, the demand for it rises and falls with popular mores. Porn became a significant part of American popular culture in 1972 with the release of *Deep Throat, Behind the Green Door*, and *The Devil in Miss Jones*. By 1977, however, porn chic was fading and the U.S. market stayed relatively limp until the beginning of the Clinton era. Aside from those started under President George Bush, federal obscenity prosecutions dropped dramatically under President Bill Clinton's Justice Department. Retired FBI agent Bill Kelly, the mastermind of MIPORN, wrote about south Florida in the spring 1997 issue of *Morality in Media*, claiming that the area symbolizes the state of the nation:

> Obscenity matters are either in a low-priority or no-priority condition, with neither law enforcement nor prosecutors moving these cases forward. While most federal and state courts have held that the judge or jury in an obscenity case must acquit if the particular hardcore video is "accepted" by the community, it would appear that in much of South Florida, the test being used by prosecutors is whether porn is "tolerated" by the community—a test that has little if anything to do with "standards of decency" that clearly favor the porn merchants.[12]

The porn industry boomed under Clinton. In 1996, according to the February 10, 1997, *U.S. News & World Report*, Americans spent more than $8 billion on porn videos, peep shows, adult cable fare, sex devices, computer porn, and sex magazines—an amount equal to Hollywood's domestic box office receipts and all the revenues generated by rock and country music recording.[13] In late 1997, *AVN* reported that sales and rentals of porn tapes had doubled over the past five years to a present gross of $5 billion a year.[14]

Patrick Trueman, who served under President George Bush as chief of the U.S. Justice Department's Exploitation and Obscenity section, maintains "the war is over. The pornographer has won."[15] Now a director of government affairs for the American Family Association, an antiporn group based in Tupelo, Mississippi, Trueman says, "These businesses in Los Angeles know they can ship around the country because no one is coming after them. If you don't bring the cases, then you, Mr. U.S. Attorney, are setting the community standard—and the community standard is anything goes."[16]

Though local branches of law enforcement usually follow the federal government's direction in prosecuting obscenity, numerous municipalities during the 1990s fought back against porn through zoning decisions that outlawed numerous sex shops and strip clubs. The most famous example is New York City, where Rudolph Giuliani, the Italian-American who led the government's onslaught against organized crime, became mayor in 1994. He cracked down on the sex industry, and in a series of court cases, defeated his pornographer and civil libertarian opponents. Times Square, once notorious for sleaze, is now safe for families. "New York City's government is acting against the pollution of the social atmosphere," wrote columnist George Will in *Newsweek*. "The city says those effects [of pornography] include decreased property values, retarded economic development, damage to neighborhood character and to children. Selling pornography . . . contributes to the coarsening of the culture which erodes civility."[17]

Columnist Don Boyett, who served on the *Orlando Sentinel*'s editorial board for years, remembers property owners pleading for support to clean up South Orange Blossom Trail, filled with crime, strip joints, and porn shops. The owners' primary interest: crime and plummeting property values.

Drive into Seminole County from the south on U.S. Highway
17-92 and what is the first thing that hits you? A large billboard
advertising a nude bar's clothing boutique. . . . Next thing you
notice are blaring signs in front of scrub parlors, nudie bars and
clearly non-family video shops. Is this the sort of seedy community you would invest in? Would that picture cause you to say,
"Hey, I'd like to live in this community?"

Those who live and own traditional businesses in that area
now are concerned. It's not just property values. They know
porn brings drugs; drugs bring other crimes. Most people don't
want to live near enterprises considered sordid. Not even the
owners of those businesses live next door. [18]

Politicians, civic leaders, citizen groups, and law enforcement
tend to agree that adult bookstores increase crime and cause
neighborhoods to deteriorate. Porn does to the community
what the religious have long argued that it does to the soul—
diminish, divide, and destroy.

Though porn is declining in some American cities such as New
York, overall it is more widely available than ever, not just in
the States but across the world, thanks to the Internet. "While
many other web outposts are flailing," writes the *Wall Street
Journal,* "adult sites are taking in millions of dollars a month.
Find a web site that is in the black and, chances are, its business and content are distinctly blue."[19] X-rated sites, which frequently advertise bestiality, defecation, child sex, and bondage,
mirror the state of porn during the less-regulated 1970s.
Because anyone can throw up a site, the net more closely
reflects what porn consumers want than do videos, which, particularly in America, voluntarily restrict their wildness. Like
their exploitation forebears, adult webmasters often exaggerate
the nastiness of their offerings: "Teen Animal Fuck, Underage

Teeny Girls, Free Hardcore Teens Do Their Dogs, Free Raped Teens, Cute Pre-Teens From Japan . . ."[20]

Porn has long led the way in the popular application of new communication technology. Many of the first novels were pornographic, such as *Fanny Hill*, which appeared eight years after the first English novel in 1640. Among the first moving pictures was an 1896 stag film. In 1973, pornographers seized the opportunity provided by cable TV's public access channels to produce raunchy shows such as *Ugly George*—whose title character goes around New York with a camera asking women to undress—and *Midnight Blue*, produced by *Screw* magazine publisher Al Goldstein. Shortly after videocassette recorders (VCRs) began selling to consumers in 1975, porn became the first industry to widely distribute its product on the new medium, even though only one home in a thousand at the time owned a VCR. Through 1983, X-rated videos accounted for three-quarters of all rentals and sales of videotapes. Another, less recognized "porn" outlet is the telephone. After the break-up of Bell's monopoly on long-distance calling, in 1983 purveyors of phone sex developed pay-per-call services.[21]

Around the same time, the French developed a prototype of the information highway known as the Internet. The government provided homes with a terminal connected to a nationwide computer system and hired academics to study "the wholesome things people would do with the terminals, like check classified ads or railroad schedules," writes Harold Rheingold in his book *The Virtual Community*. "To their utter amazement, what the French really wanted to do was talk dirty. When the network started up, the first summer they spent such an amazing amount of time typing X-rated messages to one another that they overloaded the system and brought the network down."[22]

Why is pornography so closely linked to new communication technologies? Because porn taps into insatiable desires. Men particularly long for an infinite variety of sex partners. The yearning for porn is "always unsatisfied," says Walter Kendrick, author of the 1987 book *The Secret Museum: Pornography in Modern Culture.*

> It's always a substitute for the contact between two bodies, so there's a drive behind it that doesn't exist in other genres.
>
> If you look at the history of pornography and new technologies, the track record has been pretty good. Usually everyone has come out ahead. The pornography people have gotten what they want, which is a more vivid way of portraying sex. And the technology has benefited from their experimentation. The need for innovation in pornography is so great that it usually gets to a new medium first and finds out what can be done and what can't.[23]

Despite improvements in technology, not much has changed for the better since Woody Allen said "There are three things wrong with pornographic movies—they're immoral, they're degrading and the lighting is terrible" two decades ago.[24] Though porn often leads the way in applying new technology, the quality of the final product is low. While knocking out their videos, usually in a day each, pornographers repeat the mantra "It's just a fuckin' porno" to many technical suggestions from their crew.[25]

Productions are quick and nasty for two main reasons: legal difficulties in selling porn interstate and the disappearance of adult theaters. In 1978, the height of the Golden Age, porners made about one hundred hardcore movies at a typical cost of a million 1997 dollars. It's doubtful that even one porn movie during the 1990s was made for half that much. Instead of one hundred sex flicks, however, in 1997 more than 8,000 new releases were produced, many of them made for just a few thousand dollars each. Tapes that sell more than 1,800 units are usually considered successful.[26]

The 1997 mainstream movie *Boogie Nights* portrays the dramatic changes wrought in porn by videotape. In the 1970s, production of porn was difficult and expensive because it had to be shot on film. Sales were easy, however. Now, with the declining price of video cameras, anyone can make a porno. Retailing, however, is difficult due to the increasing thicket of government regulation. "It is almost impossible to find a location for an all-adult store," writes porn attorney Clyde DeWitt in *AVN*, "and if you find a location, you have a fight against doors-off regulations, impossible licensing requirements, emergency ordinances and other operational limitations."[27] Hence, few producers make a video and try to sell it. Instead, they first get a budget and a check from a production or distribution company. (Many companies, such as VCA and Vivid, both produce and distribute porn.)

Porn retailing in Canada faces similar difficulties. Entrepreneur Randy Jorgenson, however, has surmounted most of them. Since founding Adults Only Video in 1987 as a single outlet in Saskatchewan, Jorgensen has developed a company with 500 employees, annual sales of $25 million, and eighty stores stretching from Kingston, Ontario, to Victoria, British Columbia. "Most people think of adult video stores as sleazy, back-alley operations patronized by dirty old men in trench coats," says Jorgensen. "But image is important to us. Many of our customers are well-educated people with lots of disposable income. Our stores are designed to make them feel comfortable."[28]

"Jorgensen markets hardcore films and magazines the way other businessmen sell fast food and kid's clothing," writes the Canadian newsweekly *Macleans*. "Located mostly in strip malls, the Adults Only stores bring dirty movies into the clean streets of middle-class Canada. They are the most visible sign of a spreading trend—pornography in the home."[29]

❖❖❖❖

Most Southeast Asian porn comes from Japan, which boasts a $10-billion-a-year industry that produces over 10,000 sex videos annually. The most sophisticated distribution system in the world sells the product via video and grocery stores and vending machines. "The Japanese get their cheap sex from foreigners, then come home and have normal relations with their own kind," says porn critic Max Volume. "Japan was lucky enough to keep Christianity and Freud out of their country, which probably has a lot to do with them being much more casual about sex."[30]

A typical Japanese sex shop features walls of videos depicting teenage schoolgirls, enemas, urination, and bestiality. Though Japanese law forbids display of pubic hair, most sex videos are available under the counter for $100 American.[31]

The typical male performer earns $100 per pop shot while the women earn up to $6,000 a day. Unlike the American industry, Japanese porn does not regularly test performers for HIV.[32]

❖❖❖❖

Porn tastes vary around the world. While the Japanese appear most interested in youth, the Germans in pain and pissing, and the British in schoolboy punishment, Americans seem obsessed with size—big breasts and big dicks. To satisfy these insatiable desires, pornographers like Sweden's Private (which recently went public in the United States and

Europe) travel the world in search of beautiful women willing to fornicate in front of the camera. Porn locations provide a way to measure a country's freedom. If an X-rated video is shot openly in a particular nation, there is liberty in that country. Freedom to have sex on film apparently goes hand-in-groin with freedom of speech. For example, since the end of Apartheid, one can videotape sex in South Africa as well as sell explicit videos, but few other places in Africa are as open. Popular Asian locations include Thailand and the Philippines because of their attractive women and scenery and low currency values, but you can't make porn in Communist North Korea or China.

Budapest, Hungary, is the new European center for the production of porno. After Communism's collapse in 1989, Hungarians explored the limits of freedom. Says former Foreign Minister Geza Jeszenszky, "People hated the restrictions and rushed to obtain formerly forbidden fruits, including pornography." Hungary produces about 150 sex films a year, about 10 percent of Europe's total.[33]

"But the Hungarian porn business has a sinister side," writes *Time* magazine. "Young children—usually homeless or neglected by their parents—are being lured off the streets with promises of glamorous careers in modeling. It's only later—often too late—that they learn what they're really required to do. In the provincial town of Eger in northern Hungary, a man was arrested last June for featuring girls between the ages of 10 and 15 in his pornographic films."[34]

Depending on the country, European productions can show anything—from bestiality to urination to bondage videos featuring hardcore sex. England and Ireland are the most censorious. Both cut scenes considered too sexy from mainstream movies and no X is allowed. While Ireland is sensitive to blasphemy (Monty Python's *Life of Brian* didn't make the cut), violence in film is fine. Sweden rejected the violent Belgian film *Man Bites Dog*, but it has no barriers to sexual content. Germany and Holland have little censorship. Says Pat Kelly of the *Europa Times*, "This liberal system confounds its critics by pointing out that despite a lack of censorious control, Holland has a lower crime rate than many of its counterparts with strict film guidelines." Spain, Europe's second biggest porn consumer, and Portugal have no censorship laws.[35]

Less than 10 percent of American porn is saleable in Europe because of its poor technical quality. *AVN* writes,

> Domestic producers of adult films and videos, who once depended on selling their titles to European countries for huge profits, are discovering that a large glut of product is forcing prices down, making much of their product unwanted in many countries across the pond. American pornography, once the staple diet of consumers in Germany, France, Spain and the like, has been displaced by the quality production values and sexual heat of Sweden's Private Video . . . Germany's Moli Exclusive line of high-budget features, big Italian productions such as *Marco Polo* and an unlimited supply of European product that covers the broad spectrum of sexual tastes.[36]

In Denmark, the Theander brothers own the largest porn publishing house in the world, while partners Becke Uhe and Hans Maer pour out product from Germany. Sweden's Private—founded first as a porn magazine by Berthe Milton—produces much of the world's finest porn, combining lush photography with fresh girls and nasty sex.

Milton began publishing *Private* magazine in 1966. Content with the magazine's slow but steady growth, Berthe in 1990 had only four employees—one for each edition of his magazine published each year. Then he handed over control of his company to his son, who overflowed with new ideas.

Berthe Milton the younger started a videotape line based around *Private*'s worldwide success. Each issue of *Private Video Magazine* features six to eight sexual vignettes. Next came Private Films—full-length video features of reckless sex taped in beautiful locations around the world, including Costa Rica, Thailand, and Australia.

In porn as in food, Europeans, by contrast to Americans, prefer quality over quantity. They will pay more for better product. Since 1986, the finest hardcore has come from Europe.

Conclusion

Prior to *Deep Throat* porn touched few lives and fewer societies. Since Linda Lovelace, however, the genre has demanded a share of the entertainment dollar equal to popular music and movies.

Where does porn's importance lie today? Certainly not in the arts, for porn has not produced excellent movies, books, or magazines. Nor has it created a philosophy, a politics, or a sustainable way of life.

So why study porn? What can we learn about ourselves and our civilization from the last five editions of *The Devil in Miss Jones*?

You'll have to go somewhere else to find answers to these questions. I've sought over the past ten chapters to lay out empirical truth. Moral and artistic truth, however, lies in a dimension far removed from *Anal Agony*.

Notes

1. John Johnson, "Demand Is Strong, but Police Crackdown and a Saturated Market Spell Trouble for One of L.A.'s Biggest Businesses," *Los Angeles Times Magazine*, January 17, 1991.

2. Ibid.

3. Ibid.

4. Ibid.

5. Personal interview with Ron Jeremy, June 1996.

6. John Johnson and Michael Connelly, "Killing of a Porn Pioneer Still Baffles Police," *Los Angeles Times*, August 20, 1989.

7. Ibid.

8. "King of Clubs," *Detroit News*, October 20, 1991.

9. Ibid.

10. Ibid.

11. Eric Schlosser, "The Business of Pornography," *U.S. News & World Report* (February 10, 1997): 52.

12. Bill Kelly, "Obscenity Enforcement Law Priority," *Morality in Media* (Spring 1997): 5.

13. Schlosser, "The Business of Pornography."

14. *AVN 1998 Entertainment Guide*, p. 27.

15. Jamie Dettmar, "Fight against Pornography Lags amidst Justice Scandal," *Insight* (July 22, 1996): 7.

16. Ibid.

17. George Will, "My Turn," *Newsweek* (November 11, 1996).

18. Don Boyett, "Our County," *Orlando Sentinel*, June 5, 1997.

19. Thomas E. Weber, "The X Files," *Wall Street Journal*, May 20, 1997.

20. Ads in Internet newsgrous such as alt.sex.movies.

21. John Tierney, "Sex Sells," *Baltimore Sun*, July 23, 1995.

22. Harold Rheingold, *The Virtual Community* (New York: HarperCollins, 1993), p. 54.

23. Walter Kendrick, *The Secret Museum: Pornography in Modern Culture*, quoted in Tierney, "Sex Sells."

24. Quoted on the web site www.rame.net.

25. Overheard by author during his visits to porn sets.

26. From the FAQ (Frequently Asked Questions) at the web site www.rame.net.

27. Clyde DeWitt, "Legal Commentary," *Adult Video News* (January 1998): 322.

28. D'Arcy Jenish, "The King of Porn," *Macleans* (October 11, 1993).

29. Ibid.

30. Max Volume Internet post to RAME (rec.arts.movies.erotica), April 1997.

31. Karl Taro Greenfield, *Speed Tribes* (New York: Harper Perennial, 1994), p. 143.

32. Ibid.

33. James Geary, "Sex, Lies, and Budapest," *Time International* (March 24, 1997): 72.

34. Ibid.

35. Paul Fishbein, "American Adult in Europe," *Adult Video News* (September 1994): 181.

36. Ibid.

Bibliography

Adam Film World 1996 Directory.

Adult Video News Entertainment Guide. 1997 and 1998.

Albo, Michael Louis. "Alexandra Quinn," *Hustler Erotic Video Guide* (November 1996): 45–48.

"American Garter," *Hustler Erotic Video Guide* (October 1993): 22.

"Annette Haven," *Adam Film World* (March 1987): 59.

Arcand, Bernard. *The Jaguar and the Anteater.* New York: Verso. 1993.

Armstrong, Bob. in *Exotica* (February 1997): 53.

"Blacks in Porn," *Adam Film World* (June 1983): 24–28.

Boyett, Don. "Our County." *Orlando Sentinel,* June 5, 1997.

Brent, Steve, and Elizabeth Brent. *Couples Guide to the Best Erotic Videos.* New York: St. Martin's Press, 1997.

Bright, Susie. "The Prince of Porn." *Playboy* (October 1994): 42–45.

Butler, Jerry. *Raw Talent.* Amherst, N.Y.: Prometheus Books. 1990.

Campbell, Bebe M. "A Portrait of Angel," *Essence* (November 1990): 250.

Capeci, Jerry, and Gene Mustain. *Murder Machine*. New York: Onyx, 1993.

Chapple, Steve, and David Talbot. *Burning Desires: Sex in America, A Report from the Field*. New York: Signet, 1990.

Chenery, Susan. "After the Fall," *Sydney Morning Herald*, July 15, 1995.

Cohen, Angela, and Sarah Gardner Fox. *Wise Woman's Guide to Erotic Videos*. New York: Broadway Books, 1997.

Cohn, Lawrence. "Pornmakers Surface in Mainstream." *Variety* (March 9, 1988): 3–26.

"Constance Money," *Adam* (May 1980): 17.

Cook, James. "The X-Rated Economy," *Forbes* (September 18, 1978).

Cummings, John, and Ernest Volkman. *Goombata*. Boston: Little, Brown, 1992.

Dannen, Fredric. *Hit Men*. New York: Random House, 1990.

Davis, John. *Mafia Dynasty*. New York: HarperCollins, 1993.

Denfield, Rene. *The New Victorians*. New York: Warner Books, 1995.

Dettmer, Jamie. "Fight against Pornography Lags amidst Justice Scandal," *Insight* (July 22, 1996).

DeWitt, Clyde. "Legal Commentary," *Adult Video News* (January 1998): 322.

Di Lauro, Al, and Gerald Rabkin. *Dirty Movies*. New York: Chelsea House, 1976.

Dougherty, Steve, and Dirk Mathison. "Born Again Porn Star," *People* (May 13, 1991).

Faris, Daniel, and Eddie Muller. *Grindhouse*. New York: St. Martin's Press, 1996.

Farley, Ellen and William K. Knoedelseder Jr. "The Pornbrokers," *Los Angeles Times*, June 13, 20, and 27, 1982.

Feldman, Paul, and Ronald L. Soble, "Sex Film Star Not Facing Charges," *Los Angeles Times*, July 19, 1986.

Fishbein, Paul. "American Adult in Europe," *Adult Video News* (September 1994): 181–83.

Flynt, Larry. *An Unseemly Man.* Los Angeles: Dove Books, 1996.

Ford, Luke. "AIDS," http://www.lukeford.com/d63.html (July 1998).

———. "Dead Porn Stars." http://www.lukeford.com/d46.html (January 1999).

———."Fem Porn," http://www.lukeford.com/64.html (October 1997).

"France Discovers Porn," *Oui* (April, 1976): 82–91.

Gaffin, Harris. *Hollywood Blue.* London: B. T. Batsford Ltd., 1997.

Gage, Nicholas. "Organized Crime Reaps Huge Profits from Dealing in Pornographic Films," *New York Times,* October 12, 1975. 1:1.

Geary, James. "Sex, Lies and Budapest." *Time International* (March 24, 1997): 72.

"Georgina Spelvin." *Adam Film World* (January 1987).

Greenfield, Karl Taro. *Speed Tribes.* New York: Harper Perennial, 1994.

Grey, Rudolph. *Nightmare of Ecstasy.* Los Angeles: Feral House, 1992.

Hebditch, David, and Nick Anning. *Porn Gold.* London: Faber & Faber, 1988.

Heidenry, John. *What Wild Ecstasy: The Rise and Fall of the Sexual Revolution.* New York: Simon & Schuster, 1997.

"Here Cums Samantha Fox," *Swank* (June 1987): 43.

Holliday, Jim. "Oh Boy, Oh Joy, Another Gang Bang Movie," *Adult Video News* (September 1996): 68.

Holliday, Jim. *Only the Best.* Van Nuys, Calif.: Cal Vista Direct Ltd. 1986.

Hubner, John. *Bottom Feeders.* New York: Doubleday, 1992.

"In the Realm of the Senses," *Magill's Survey of Cinema* (June 15, 1995).

"An Interview with Howard Ziehm," *Screw* (September 30, 1974).

Isherwood, Charles. *Wonder Bread and Ecstasy: The Life and Death of Joey Stefano.* Los Angeles: Alyson Publications Inc., 1996.

"Jamie Gillis Teaches 'Porn Shooting for Beginners' Course," *Adult Video News* (September 1994): 54.

Jenish, D'Arcy. "The King of Porn," *Macleans* (October 11, 1993): 52–57.

"Jesie St. James," *Adam* (May 1980): 12–14.

Johnson, John. "Demand Is Strong, but Police Crackdown and a Saturated Market Spell Trouble for One of L.A.'s Biggest Businesses," *Los Angeles Times Magazine* (February 17, 1991).

Johnson, John, and Michael Connelly. "Killing of a Porn Pioneer Still Baffles Police," *Los Angeles Times*, August 20, 1989.

Johnson, Paul. *A History of the Jews*. New York: HarperCollins, 1988.

Jordan, Pat. "Traci Lords with Her Clothes On," *GQ* (April 1990): 250–55.

Kelly, Bill. "Obscenity Enforcement Low Priority," *Morality in Media* (Spring 1997): 5.

"Kelly Nichols," *Adam* (October 1993): 18.

Kendrick, Walter. *The Secret Museum*. New York: Viking Penguin Inc., 1987.

Kennedy, Dana. "Up Front and Personal: Cult Director Russ Meyer," *Entertainment Weekly* (April 5, 1996): 90.

"King of Clubs," *Detroit News*, October 20, 1991, 1:1.

Kristol, Irving. *Reflections of a Neoconservative*. New York: Basic Books, 1983.

Kurins, Andris, and Joseph F. O'Brien. *Boss of Bosses*. New York: Island Books, 1991.

Kutchinsky, Berl. *Encyclopedia of Crime and Justice*. New York: Free Press, 1983.

Lenne, Gerard. *Sex on the Screen*. New York: St. Martin's Press, 1978.

"Linda Lovelace's Ordeal," *Toronto Sun*, March 20, 1981.

Linedecker, Clifford L. *Children in Chains*. New York: Everest House, 1981.

Lorenz, Jay Kent. "The Erotic World of Radley Metzger," *Psychotronic Video*, issue 17 (Winter 1994).

Lovelace, Linda. *Out of Bondage*. New York: Berkley Books, 1986.

Lovelace, Linda, with Mike McGrady. *Ordeal*. (New York: Berkley Books, 1980).

Malinowski, W. Zachary. "R.I. Pornographer Pleads Guilty," *Providence Journal-Bulletin*, January 11, 1997.

Margold, Bill. "The Private Afternoons of Pamela Mann," *Hollywood Press* (April 1975): 21.

———. "Sex and Violence," *Hollywood Press* (October 1975): 34.

"Max Hardcore 10: High Voltage," *Adult Video News* (February 1995): 134

McCumber, David. *X-Rated*. New York: Simon & Schuster, 1992.

McDonagh, Maitland. *The 50 Most Erotic Films of All Time*. New York: Citadel Press, 1996.

McGrady, Mike. *Stranger Than Naked or How to Write Dirty Books for Fun & Profit*. New York: Lyle Stuart, 1970.

Michael Satchell. "The Big Business of Selling Smut," *Parade* (August 19, 1979).

Mithers, Carol Lynn. "She Works Hard for the Money: Portrait of a Porn Star," *Mademoiselle* (November 1985): 172–73.

"Neighborhood Porn Wars," *Newsday*, April 18, 1993.

Peterson, Clarence. "Porn? Rate it 'Ex' for Marilyn Chambers," *Chicago Tribune*, June 2, 1989.

Peterson, James R. "A History of Sex in the 1930s," *Playboy* (August 1997): 146.

Petkovich, Anthony. *The X Factory*. Manchester: Headpress, 1997.

Point, Jack. "Adult Goes Airborne," *Adult Video News* (October 1994): 163.

"Porn Talk," *Puritan*, no. 8 (1984).

"The Porno Plague," *Men's Perspective*, issue 1 (1996): 145–52.

"The Porno Plague," *Time* (April 5, 1976): 58–63.

Potter, Gary. *The Porn Merchants*. Dubuque: Kendall Hunt, 1986.

Prager, Dennis, and Joseph Telushkin. *Why the Jews: The Reason for Antisemitism*. New York: Simon & Schuster, 1983.

Ravo, Nick. "The Core of Paul Little." *Icon* (February 1997): 100–109.

The Report of the Commission on Obscenity and Pornography. New York: Bantam Books, 1970.

Rheingold, Harold. *The Virtual Community.* New York: Harper-Collins, 1993.

Riley, Pat. *X-Rated Videotape Guide IV.* Amherst, N.Y.: Prometheus Books, 1996).

Rimmer, Robert. *The X-Rated Videotape Guide.* Amherst, N.Y.: Prometheus Books, 1993.

———. *X-Rated Videotape Guide II.* Amherst, N.Y.: Prometheus Books, 1991.

Rotsler, William. *Contemporary Erotic Cinema.* New York: Penthouse/Ballantine, 1973.

Sager, Mike. "The Devil and John Holmes," *Rolling Stone* (June 15, 1989): 50–67.

Schlosser, Eric. "The Business of Pornography," *U.S. News & World Report* (February 10, 1997): 42–52.

Schatz, Carol, and Lorenzo Benet. "Sequel: Porn Free More Than 20 Years after 'The Devil in Miss Jones,' Georgina Spelvin Is Dried Out and Demonless," *People* (March 13, 1995): 91–92.

Schmich, Mary T. "Star of Film Fantasies Satisfied Staying Dressed for Success," *Chicago Tribune*, October 11, 1985.

Slade, Joseph W. "The Porn Market and Porn Formulas: The Feature Film of the Seventies," *Journal of Popular Culture* 6, no. 2: 168–86.

"Smart Aleck Candy Barr," *Oui* (April 1976): 75.

Smith, Kent. "In Love," *Adam* (October 1983): 32.

Sneed, Michael, and Kathy O'Malley. "Rob and Ginger and Rona," *Chicago Tribune*, March 14, 1986.

Snowden, Lynn. "A Prude's Guide to Erotica," *Cosmopolitan* (May 1993): 82–84.

Stanley, Lawrence A. "The Child Porn Myth," *Cardoza Arts and Entertainment Law Review* (1989): 295–330.

Stanmeyer, William A. *The Seduction of Society.* Ann Arbor, Mich.: Servant Publications, 1984.

Stoller, Robert. *Porn.* New Haven: Yale University Press, 1991.

———. *Sexual Excitement: The Dynamics of Erotic Life*. New York: Pantheon Books, 1979.

Stoller, Robert, and Ira Levine. *Coming Attractions*. New Haven: Yale University Press, 1993.

Svetkey, Benjamin. "Oral Argument," *Entertainment Weekly* (February 26, 1993): 68.

Talese, Gay. *Thy Neighbor's Wife*. New York: Doubleday, 1980.

Teachout, Terry. "The Pornography Report That Never Was," *Commentary* (August 1987): 51–55.

Tierney, John. "Sex Sells," *Baltimore Sun*, July 23, 1995.

Trist, N. P. "Why Porn Is Legal in California," ASM (alt.sex. movies) library, http://home.eznet.net/~rwilhelm/asm/library/essays/porn-legal-ca.html (October 13, 1995).

Turan, Kenneth, and Stephen F. Zito. *Sinema*. New York: Praeger Publishers, 1974.

U.S. Department of Justice, Attorney General's Commission on Pornography, Final Report. Washington D.C.: U.S. Government Printing Office, 1986.

United States v. *Thevis*, 665 F. 2d 616 (5th Cir. 1982).

"Vanessa Del Rio," *Adam* (May 1980): 38.

Weber, Thomas E. "The X Files," *Wall Street Journal*, May 20, 1997.

Wilke, John R. "Porn Broker," *Wall Street Journal*, July 11, 1994.

Will, George. "My Turn," *Newsweek*, November 11, 1996.

Williams, Linda *Hard Core: Power, Pleasure, and the 'Frenzy of the Visible*. Berkeley: University of California Press, 1989.

Williamson, Bruce. "Porn Stars," *Playboy* (October 1974): 72–74.

Wilson, James Q., and Richard Hernstein. *Crime and Human Nature*. New York: Simon & Schuster, 1985.

Wolcott, James. "A Walk on the Dark Side," *Vanity Fair* (March 1987): 30–31.

Ziplow, Stephen. *The Film Maker's Guide to Pornography*. New York: Drake, 1977.

Zorn, Eric. "Seka Can't Seem to Find Big Time," *Chicago Tribune*, November 17, 1992.

Zuckerman, Michael J. *Vengeance Is Mine.* New York: MacMillian, 1987.

Index